Lucius D. Gould

**The Carpenter's and Builder's Assistant**

And Wood Worker's Guide

Lucius D. Gould

**The Carpenter's and Builder's Assistant**
*And Wood Worker's Guide*

ISBN/EAN: 9783337060282

Printed in Europe, USA, Canada, Australia, Japan

Cover: Foto ©Andreas Hilbeck / pixelio.de

More available books at **www.hansebooks.com**

# THE

# CARPENTER'S AND BUILDER'S

## ASSISTANT,

AND

# WOOD WORKER'S

## GUIDE.

BY LUCIUS D. GOULD,

Architect and Practical Builder.

---

NEW YORK:
A. J. BICKNELL & CO.,
ARCHITECTURAL BOOK PUBLISHERS,
1874.

Entered according to Act of Congress in the year 1874, by
LUCIUS D. GOULD,
In the Office of the Librarian of Congress, at Washington.

DAILY ADVERTISER PRINT,
NEWARK, NEW JERSEY.

# PREFACE.

Several years have elapsed since I first published the House Carpenter's Assistant, which met with a ready sale of some seventeen hundred copies, but in consequence of the death of the publisher the work is now out of print.

The object of the author is to revise the former work by omitting the treaties on mathematical instruments, to make room for additional matter that had been overlooked in the former work, in order to furnish house carpenters and builders with a new and easy system of lines founded on geometrical principles for framing the most difficult roofs; for cutting every description of joints and for finding the sections of angular pieces at any point from a horizontal to a perpendicular, so that their sides shall be in the plane of the sides they are connected with; for finding the form of the raking mould, for a gable, to intersect with the horizontal mould at any angle diverging from a straight line; the mitreing of circular mouldings; the relative sizes of timbers framed to support a given weight; to the mitreing of planes oblique to the base at any angle.

Together with these rules, the author also presents tables of the weight and cohesive strength of the different materials used in the construction of buildings as well as the weight required to crush said materials, with a treatise on the adhesion of nails, screws, iron pins and glue. Also an easy system of stair railing for straight and platform stairs, which will enable carpenters to finish and complete a dwelling without the assistance of a professional stair builder.

And to all this is added a practical and mathematical demonstration of finding the circumference and squaring the circle when the diameter is given.

There can be but little doubt that a work of this kind is needed by architects and builders, and especially by carpenters and workmen who are inexperienced in the different kinds of labor which they are

PREFACE.

called upon to perform. Many a journeyman carpenter has found himself suddenly thrown out of employment simply because he was ignorant of the rules by which he could perform some required task. It is rather for the benefit of such than for the experienced workmen, that this volume is designed, and should it be the means of promoting their interest or inciting them to a study of the noble science and art of construction, the author will feel well compensated for his labor.

It is but due to acknowledge that we have consulted the valuable works of Thomas Tredgold, for the articles on the strength and weight of materials, also to Mr. Honetus M. Albee, a skillful and experienced stair-builder for the method of finding the distances to kerf the back string for circular stairs.

Plate 1.

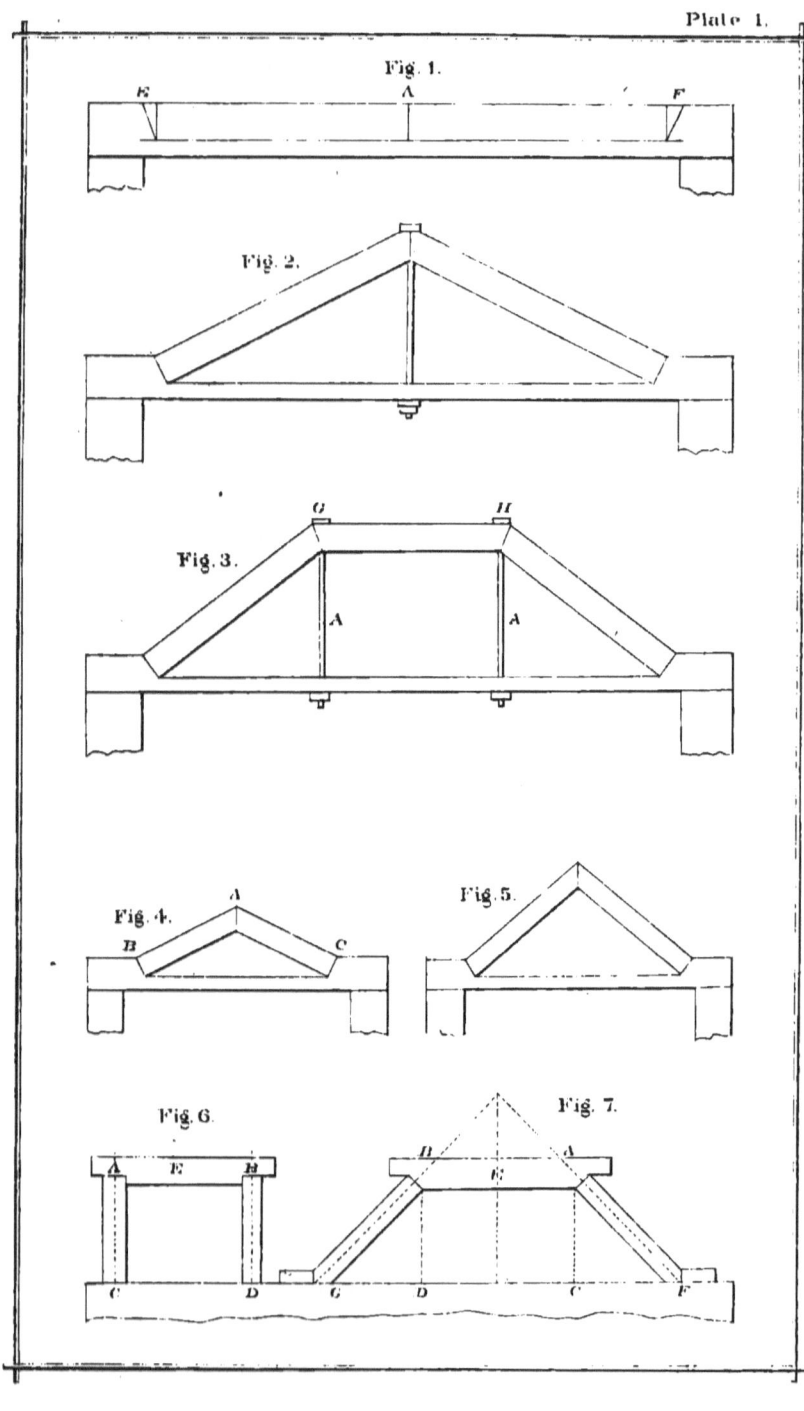

# CARPENTRY.

Carpentry is the art of cutting and jointing timbers in the construction of buildings.

To cut timbers and adapt them to their various situations, so that one of the sides of every piece shall be arranged according to a given plane or surface shown in the designs of the architect, is a department of carpentry which requires a thorough knowledge of the finding of sections of solids, their coverings and the various methods of connecting timbers, etc.

The art of combining pieces of timber to increase their strength and firmness, is called framing.

The form of a frame should be adapted to the nature of the load which it is designed to carry.

In carpentry, the load is usually distributed over the whole length of the framing, but it is generally supported from point to point, by short beams or joists.

First, let us consider a case where the load is collected at one point of the frame, and in order that the advantage of framing may be more obvious, let us suppose all the parts of a certain piece of frame work to be cut out of a single beam, which in a solid mass, would be too weak for the purpose.

## PLATE 1.

Let Fig. 1 be a piece of timber cut in the various directions indicated by the lines passing through it; and let the triangular pieces shown at E and F be removed, then raise the pieces A E and A F till they make close joints at E and F, and increase their lengths till they form a frame or truss, as represented at Fig. 2. A small rod of iron with suitable nuts, will be required to support the centre of the tie, as seen in the drawing. If the depth of the frame at the middle be double the depth of the beam, the strength of the frame will be a little more than eight times as great as that of the beam. If the depth of the frame be three times the depth of the beam as represented at Fig. 2, it will be about six times as strong as the beam, and about eighteen times as firm, that is, it will bend only an eighteenth part of the distance which the beam would bend under the same weight.

To render the strength more equal and to obtain two points of support, there may be a level piece of timber placed between the inclining ones, as shown at Fig 3; but if a greater weight be placed at G than at H, there will be a tendency to spring upwards at H and inwards at A, which may be effectually prevented by the suspension rod A A, as shown in the same figure.

It now remains to show why the strength of a piece of timber is increased by forming it into a truss; and to have a clear conception of this subject is of the utmost importance in the science of carpentry.

Let A B C Fig. 4 be a truss to support a weight applied at A. It is evident that the force of the weight will tend to spread the abutments B and C, and the nearer we make the angle A B C to a straight line, the greater will be the pressure or tendency to spread or increase at A. On the contrary, if the height be increased as at Fig. 5, the tendency to spread the abutment will be less.

The advantage of framing timbers together for the purpose of giving strength and firmness having been shown, let us proceed to explain how the strain on any part may be measured.

To find the pressure on oblique supports or parts of trusses, frames, etc. Let A B Fig. 6 be a heavy beam supported by two posts A C and B D, placed at equal distances from E, the centre of the beam. The pressure on each post will obviously be equal to half the weight of the beam. But if the posts be placed obliquely as in Fig. 7, the pressure on each post will be increased in the same proportion as its length is increased, the height A C, being the same as before; that is, when A F is double A C, the pressure on the post in the direction of its length is double the half weight of the beam. Hence it is very easy to find the pressure in the direction of an inclined strut, for it is as many times half the weight supported as A C is contained in A F. Therefore, if the depth A C of a truss to support a weight of two tons be only one foot, and A F be ten feet, the pressure in the direction of A F will be ten tons.

It will be observed that when the beam is supported by oblique posts, as in Fig. 7, these posts will slide out at the bottom and together at the top, if not prevented by proper abutments. The force with which the foot F tends to slide out is to half the weight of the beam A B, as F C is to A C. Therefore, when F C is equal to A C, the tendency to slide out is equal to half the weight supported; and if F C be ten times A C, the tendency to spread out would be ten times the weight supported. Hence it is evident that a flat truss requires a tie of immense strength to prevent it from spreading. If a flat truss produces any degree of stretching in the tie, the truss must obviously settle, and by settling it becomes flat and consequently exerts a greater strain. In a flat truss, therefore, too much caution cannot be used in fitting the joints and choosing good materials.

# PROBLEMS.

## PLATE 2.

*To form an Ellipsis by means of a cord:*—Let A B (Figure 1) be the longest diameter and D C the shortest diameter of the required ellipse. Make C F and C G equal to E B, which is one-half the longest diameter. At the points G and F place pins, around the pins place a cord so fastened at the ends that it shall reach around the points C F G; place your pencil inside the cord and describe the ellipsis. Care must be taken to keep the cord to an even tension.

FIGURE 2.—*A side of a Polygon of any number of sides being given to describe the Polygon:*—Let A B C be a line and B C the given side of a polygon of five sides. From B as a centre, with B C as a radius, describe a semi-circle and divide it into five parts; through the points of division 1, 2, draw the lines B D and B E indefinitely; then with one point of the compass at C, with C B as radius, describe the dotted circle B D, cutting the line B D at D; perpendicular to B C, draw the line C E, join 3, 1, and at the intersection of the lines 3, 1 and C E will be the centre to describe the circle B C D, etc.; join C D, etc., and the figure will be complete.

FIGURE 3.—*To describe the false ellipsis, or an elliptical figure by means of circular arcs:*—Let A B be the length and C D the breadth; join B D through the centre of the line E B, and at right angles to B D draw the line C F indefinitely; then at the points of intersection of the dotted lines will be found the points to describe the required ellipsis.

FIGURE 4.—*To inscribe an equilateral triangle in a given circle:*—Through the centre A, draw any diameter B C; from the point C as a centre, with the radius C A, describe the arc

Plate 2

Fig. 1.

Fig. 2.

Fig. 3.

Fig. 4.

Fig. 5.

Fig. 6.

D A E; join B D, B E and D E, then D B E is the equilateral-triangle required.

FIGURE 5.—*To describe a regular Octagon from a given square:*—Draw the diagonal A B, then with half the diagonal as a radius, describe from each of the four angular points of the square, the arcs cutting the centre and sides of the square. Join the points of intersection and the required octagon is obtained.

FIGURE 5.—*To inscribe a Polygon of six sides:*—Describe the circle as shown from the points A B with the same radius, describe the arcs within the circle. Join the points of intersection by the chords as shown and the required polygon will be obtained.

## PLATE 3.

Exhibits a plan of groin arches, designed for brick or stone materials, resting on eight piers, which are represented by the letters A B C, etc.

FIGURE 1—On the line A H of the lesser opening between two adjacent piers, describe the semi-circle A G H; divide the arc A C in any number of equal parts as shown; drop the lines from the points on the arc, at right angles to A G, cutting the diagonal lines I K in the points 1, 2, 3; etc., from the points thus found on the lines I K, draw the perpendicular lines 1 1, 2 2, etc., equal to those shown at the semi-circle A G H, and through the points 1, 2, 3, etc., describe the curve lines for the intersecting ribs, over the lines I K and L M as shown on the plan.

FIGURE 2—Shows a method of forming the curves for the intersecting rib, by using a cord as shown at Fig. 1, Plate 2.

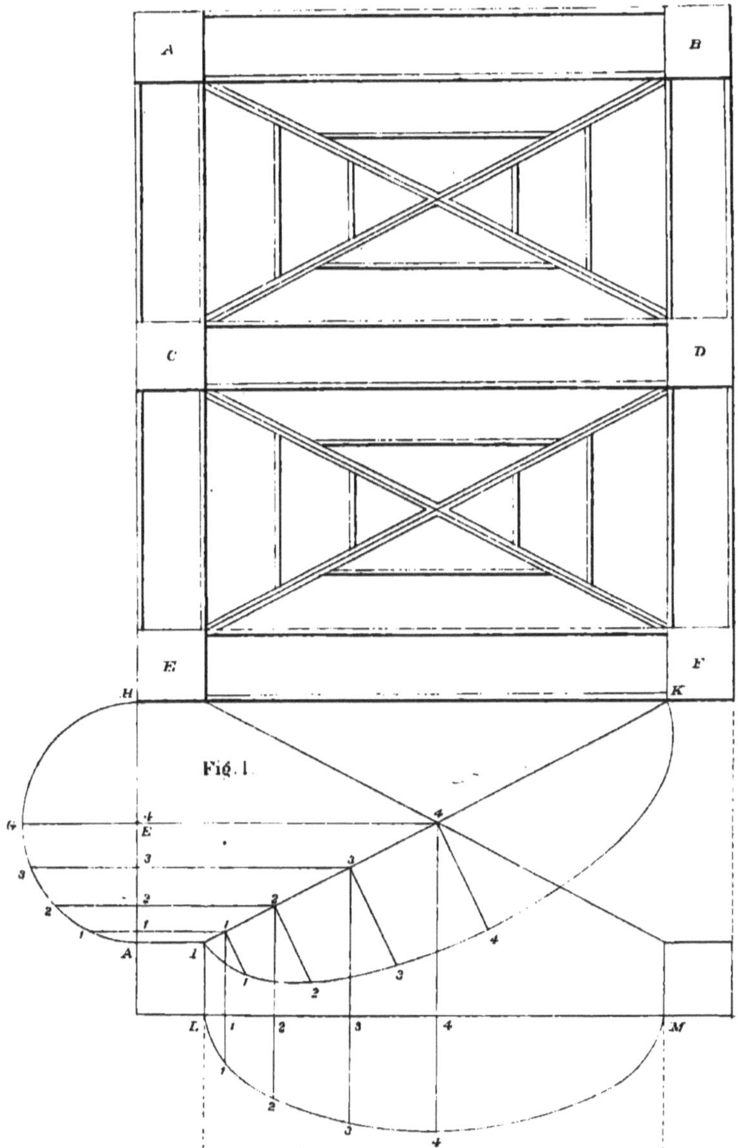

Fig. 1.

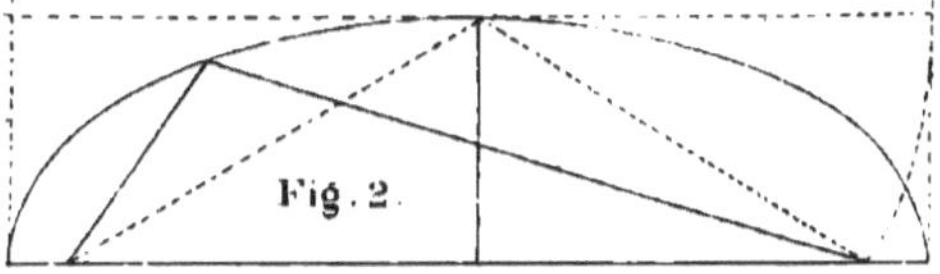

Fig. 2.

# TABLE

Showing the length of Brace when the run is given, also the length of run when the Brace is given.

| RUN. | BRACE. | BRACE. | RUN. |
|---|---|---|---|
| 2 ft.     × 2 ft.          | 2.8284  | 2 ft.       | 1.4142 × 1.4142 |
| 2 ft. 3 in. × 2 ft. 3 in.  | 3.1819  | 2 ft. 3 in. | 1.5909 × 1.5909 |
| 2 ft. 6 in. × 2 ft. 6 in.  | 3.5749  | 2 ft. 6 in. | 1.7879 × 1.7879 |
| 2 ft. 9 in. × 2 ft. 9 in.  | 3.8903  | 2 ft. 9 in. | 1.9451 × 1.9451 |
| 3 ft.     × 3 ft.          | 4.2426  | 3 ft.       | 2.1213 × 2.1213 |
| 3 ft. 3 in. × 3 ft. 3 in.  | 4.5961  | 3 ft. 3 in. | 2.2980 × 2.2980 |
| 3 ft. 6 in. × 3 ft. 6 in.  | 4.9497  | 3 ft. 6 in. | 2.4748 × 2.4748 |
| 3 ft. 9 in. × 3 ft. 9 in.  | 5.3141  | 3 ft. 9 in. | 2.6570 × 2.6570 |
| 4 ft.     × 4 ft.          | 5.6568  | 4 ft.       | 2.8784 × 2.8784 |
| 4 ft. 3 in. × 4 ft. 3 in.  | 6.0103  | 4 ft. 3 in. | 3.0051 × 3.0051 |
| 4 ft. 6 in. × 4 ft. 6 in.  | 6.3639  | 4 ft. 6 in. | 3.1819 × 3.1819 |
| 4 ft. 9 in. × 4 ft. 9 in.  | 6.7162  | 4 ft. 9 in. | 3.3581 × 3 3581 |
| 5 ft.     × 5 ft.          | 7.0705  | 5 ft.       | 3.5357 × 3.5357 |
| 5 ft. 3 in. × 5 ft. 3 in.  | 7.4246  | 5 ft. 3 in. | 3.7123 × 3.7123 |
| 5 ft. 6 in. × 5 ft. 6 in.  | 7.7781  | 5 ft. 6 in. | 3.8890 × 3.8890 |
| 5 ft 9 in. × 5 ft. 9 in.   | 8.1317  | 5 ft. 9 in. | 4.0658 × 4.0658 |
| 6 ft.     × 6 ft.          | 8.4852  | 6 ft.       | 4 2426 × 4.2426 |
| 6 ft. 3 in. × 6 ft. 3 in.  | 8.8388  | 6 ft. 3 in. | 4.4194 × 4.4194 |
| 6 ft. 6 in. × 6 ft. 3 in.  | 9.1923  | 6 ft. 6 in. | 4.5961 × 4.5961 |
| 6 ft. 9 in. × 6 ft. 9 in.  | 9.5459  | 6 ft. 9 in. | 4.7729 × 4.7729 |
| 7 ft.     × 7 ft.          | 9.9000  | 7 ft.       | 4.9500 × 4.9500 |
| 7 ft. 3 in. × 7 ft. 3 in.  | 10.2412 | 7 ft. 3 in. | 5.1206 × 5.1206 |
| 7 ft. 6 in. × 7 ft. 6 in.  | 10.8863 | 7 ft. 6 in. | 5.4431 × 5.4431 |
| 7 ft. 9 in. × 7 ft. 9 in.  | 10.9181 | 7 ft. 9 in. | 5.4590 × 5.4590 |
| 8 ft.     × 8 ft.          | 11.3132 | 8 ft.       | 5.6566 × 5.6566 |

To reduce the decimals to inches, multiply by 12 for inches, the product by 8 for eights, the eights by 2 for sixteenths. Example.

5.6566 = 5 ft. 7⅛ in.

```
   5.6566
       12
   ──────
   7.8792
        8
   ──────
   7.0336
        2
   ──────
    .0672
```

# BRACKETING.

Bracketing is the method of forming the angle between the ceiling and the side walls of a room for the lath and plaster cornice. Its form may be elliptical, or of other compound curves; and when they are large, in order to save materials, the plaster is supported on laths which are fastened to wooden brackets, placed from twelve to sixteen inches from centres; and in order to support the laths at the mitres, brackets are fixed at the internal and external angles.

## PLATE 4.

FIGURE 1.—*Shows the method of finding the bracket for an external acute angle :*—Let A C be the projection of the cove; C B the line of the side wall, B F the line of the ceiling, and B C D the given angle; produce F A to E, draw E H parallel to C D; divide the given bracket into any number of equal parts and from the points of division on the curve line, drop the lines 1, 1, 1, 2, 2, 2, etc., to the line C E; draw the line E G perpendicular to C E, and equal to A H; draw 1, 1, 2, 2, parallel to E G; make the perpendicular equal to those they are connected with on the given bracket, and through the points thus found, draw the curve of the angle rib. The dotted curve shows the bevel or splay of the bracket to form the plane that shall coincide with the plane of the given brackets.

FIGURE 2.—Exhibits the method of finding the bracket for an internal right-angle, and is precisely the same as Fig. 1, with the exception of bevelling the angle bracket which is not necessary for an internal angle.

Plate 4.

Fig. 1.

Fig. 2.

Fig. 3.

FIGURE 3.—*Shows the manner of finding the centre, or radius of a circle whose centre is lost:*—Let A B be the curve, take any points A C B with the same radius, describe the arcs as shown at D E and through the points of intersection of the arcs; draw the lines E H and G H, and where they intersect each other will be the centre of the circle, which can be proved by application of the compass.

# Development of Surfaces.

## PLATE 5.

*Springing and Bending Mouldings :*—Figures 1 and 2 show at A and B what are termed among carpenters and joiners, spring mouldings, and the stuff from which they are obtained are thinner than if the angular piece were worked on the moulding. These mouldings require brackets placed at proper distances, either in a straight or curved line. If they are curved, the moulding will require to be bent in the same manner as in covering the frustum of a right curve.

Figure 1.—Shows an elevation of a circular moulding mitered into a level moulding. The form and position is shown at A, and the workmen will perceive that by producing the line B D to intersect the centre line of the arc at C, he will have the point to describe the circular piece for the moulding required. E B and F D gives the radius for the curve of the out and inside edges, when placed in the position shown on the elevation.

Figure 2.—Shows the application of the same rules to a circular elevation of a different form standing over a straight plan. The back lines of the moulding are produced until they bisect a horizontal line drawn through the centre, from which the circular cornice was struck, as shown by the lines A B and C D. In other respects the operation is precisely the same as at Fig. 1.

Figure 3.—*A tangent to a circle being given to find the point of contact with the circle.*—Let C be the centre on which to describe the circle and A B the tangent, bisect B C, then with one point of the compass in E, with the same

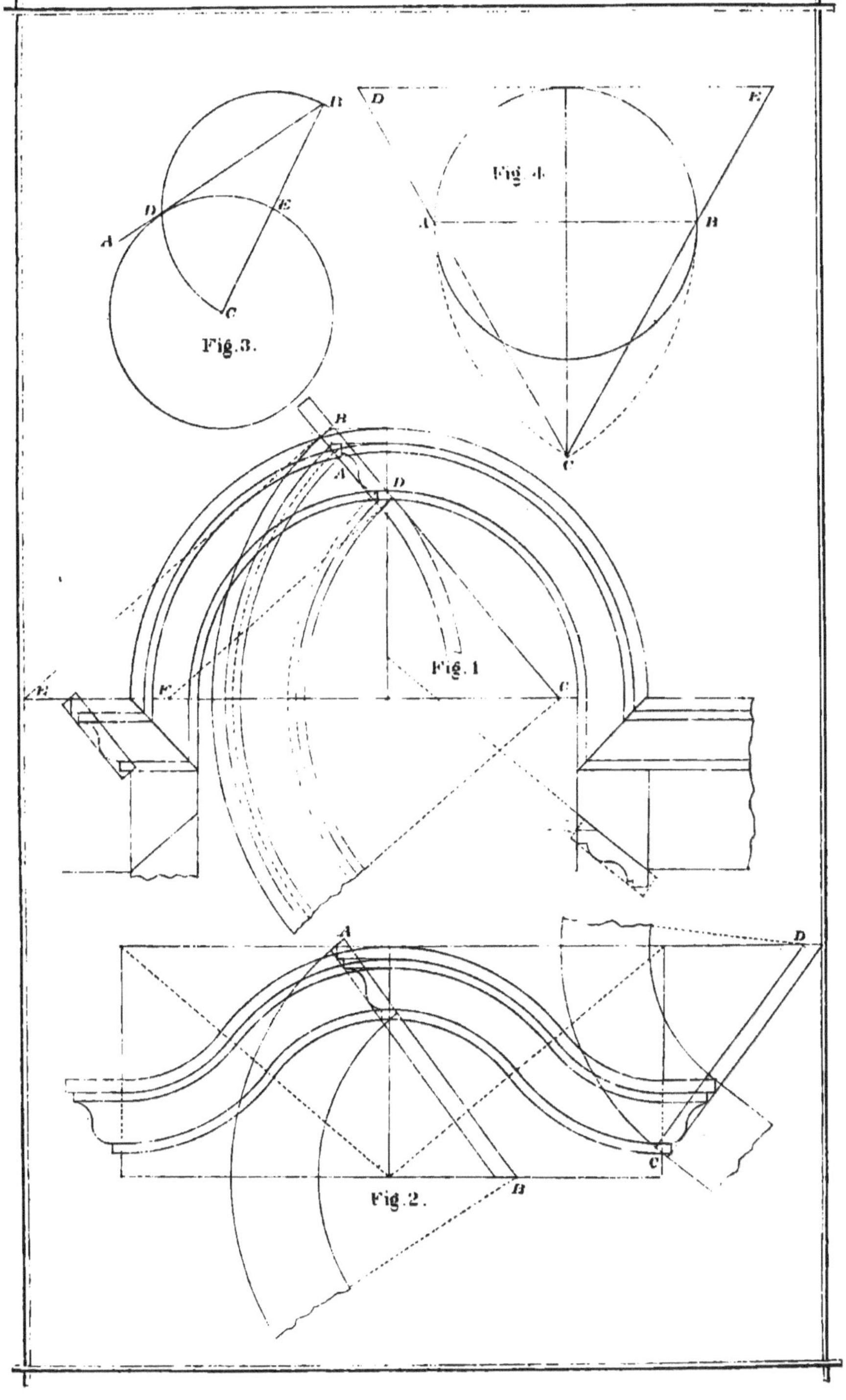

Plate 5.

Fig. 3.

Fig. 4.

Fig. 1.

Fig. 2.

radius, describe the arc B D C, then the intersection of the circular lines shown at D is the point of contact.

FIGURE 4.—*Having the diameter given to find the circumference of a circle Geometrically:*—Let A B be the given diameter; take the distance A B as a radius, and with A and B as centres, describe the arcs intersecting at C; join C A and C B, and produce them to the tangent D E, then D E will be the development, or stretch-out of half the circumference, nearly.

# CARPENTRY.

## PLATE 6.

The carpenter's square is the measure of distance, and is as important and valuable to the workman as the clock is to the time-keeper, or the compass to the mariner. The square in general use consists of a blade and tongue placed at right-angles to each other. The blade is two feet; the tongue, twelve, or sixteen inches long, divided into inches and eights of an inch. For convenience of workmen, will be seen at

FIGURE 1.—A method of dividing a board in an even number of equal parts, when the same is an uneven number of inches, or parts of an inch in width, by placing the square as shown, with the points of the square on the edges of the board; then the points of division will be found at 6, 12 and 18, for dividing the board in four equal parts.

FIGURE 2.—Exhibits a method of finding the lines for eight squaring a piece of timber with the square, by placing the blade on the piece, and making the points seven inches from the ends of the square, from which to draw the lines for the sides of the octagonal piece required. At the heel of the square is shown a method of cutting a board to fit any angle with the square and compass, by placing the square in the angle and taking the distance from the heel of the square to the angle A in the compass; then lay the square on the piece to be fitted with the distance taken, and from the point A draw the line A B, which will give the angle to cut the piece required.

FIGURE 3.—Exhibits a method of constructing a polygonal figure of eight sides; by placing the square on the line A B with equal distances on the blade and tongue, as shown; the curve lines show the method of transferring the distances; the diagonal gives the intersection at the angles.

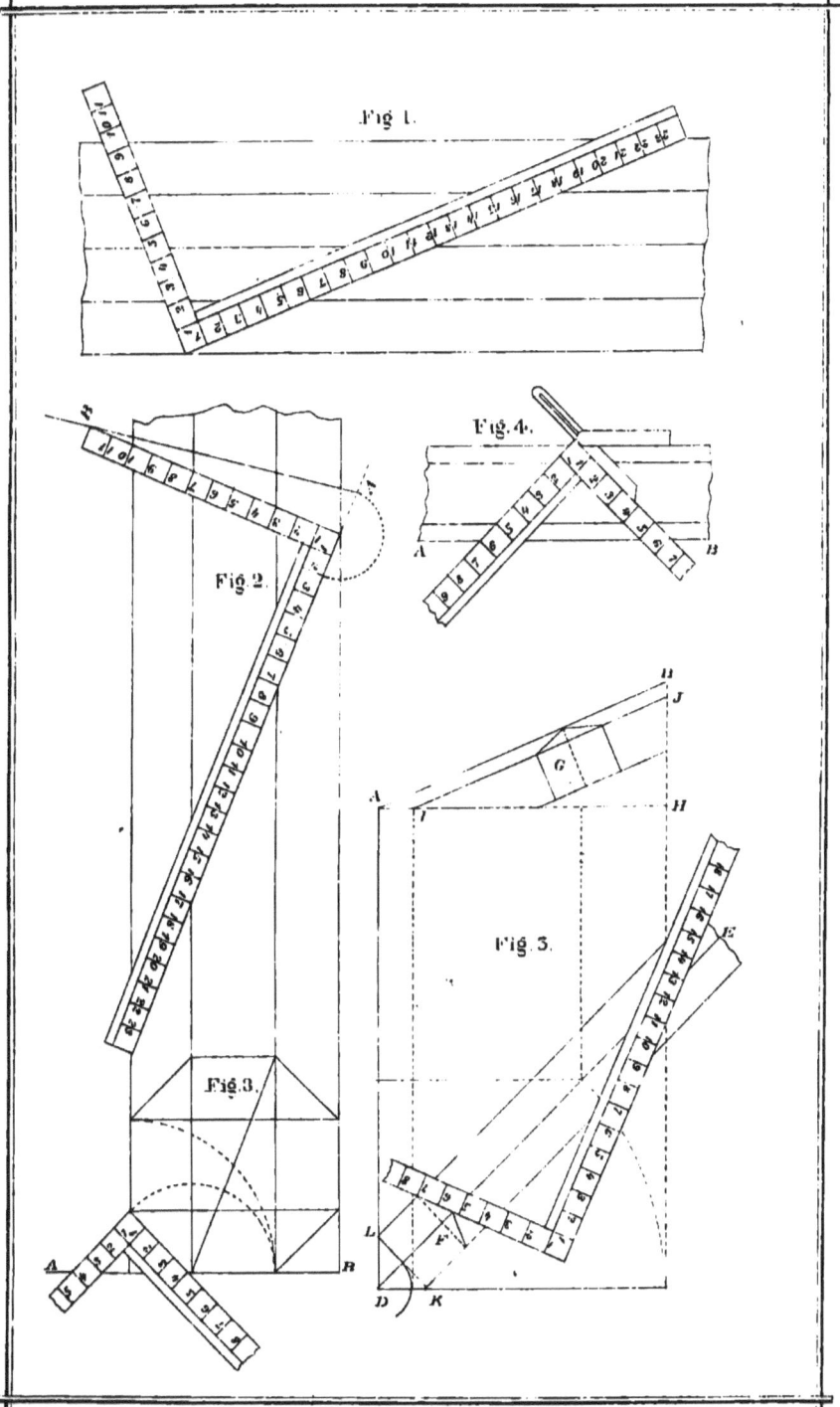

FIGURE 4.—Exhibits a method of finding the cuts in a mitre-box, by placing the square on the line A B at equal distances from the heel of the square, say six inches. The bevel is shown to prove the truth of the lines by applying it to the opposite sides of the square. To find the perpendicular and horizontal cut of rafters, with the square, take the horizontal distance, or half the width of the building for the run, on the blade, and the rise, on the tongue.

FIGURE 5.—Exhibits two methods of finding the backing of the angle or hip rafter; one, which is in Bell's Work on Carpentry Made Easy, is by taking the length of rafter on the blade and the rise or height on the tongue, and placing the square on the line D E, the plan of the hip, the angle is given to bevel the hip rafter, as shown at F. This method gives the angle to bevel the hip-rafter, only for a right-angled plan, where the pitches are the same, *and no other*, which makes it circumstantial, and of little or no value to the workman.

The other method, which is original with me, applies to right, obtuse and acute angles, where the pitches are the same. At the angle D will be seen the line from the points K L, at the intersection of the sides of the angle rafter with the sides of the plan. With one point of the compass at D, describe the curve from the line K L. Tangential to the curve draw the dotted line, cutting A H at I; draw I J parallel to A B, the pitch of the angle-rafter. At G will be found a section of the hip or angle-rafter. The rules here shown are only applicable to certain cases where the pitches are the same. But to enable the workman to construct anything that any one may design, we would refer him to the method shown on Plate 9, which is a principle that applies to the finding of sections of angular pieces to any angle, from the horizontal to the perpendicular.

## PLATE 7.

Shows a timber foundation for a frame building with two side elevations, framed in the usual manner for good houses. The object of this and the following Plates, is first to give the inexperienced workman the names used among carpenters and joiners, of the different pieces of timber used in framing and where they are placed. Also to show the method of constructing what is called a balloon frame.

FIGURE 1.—Shows a timber plan of foundation supported by brick or stone walls. The outside timbers are called sills, and if there are no openings, all other timbers are called beams; but when there are openings for chimneys or stairways, the workman will be required to mortice and tenon the timbers together, as shown on the plan. Then the first piece of timber to prepare will be the *trimmer*, shown at A, which is tenoned into the *trimmer-beams*, shown at B B. The short beams tenoned into the *trimmer* are called *tail-beams*. Fig. 2 and 3 are the front and a portion of the side elevation of the frame, standing on the foundation, showing the posts, beams, enter-ties, plates, rafters and braces, in their proper places. The timbers shown at A A, Fig. 2, are called frame-beams, D D corner posts and C C rafters. At Fig. 3, A shows what should be called an intermediate post; the pieces of timber called *enter-ties*, are shown at B B; the piece of timber supporting the rafters at C, represents the *plate*, and B B the *sills*; the oblique pieces of timber shown on the elevations, are called *braces*; the timbers shown on each side of the openings, are called *joists*, and termed door and window joist; those placed between doors and windows are called intermediate joists or *furrings*; all joists cut under or over the braces are called *cripples*; a piece of timber placed on piers for the purpose of supporting other timbers or partitions are called *summers*; a piece of timber placed on a truss frame for the purpose of supporting the common rafters, is called a *purlin*.

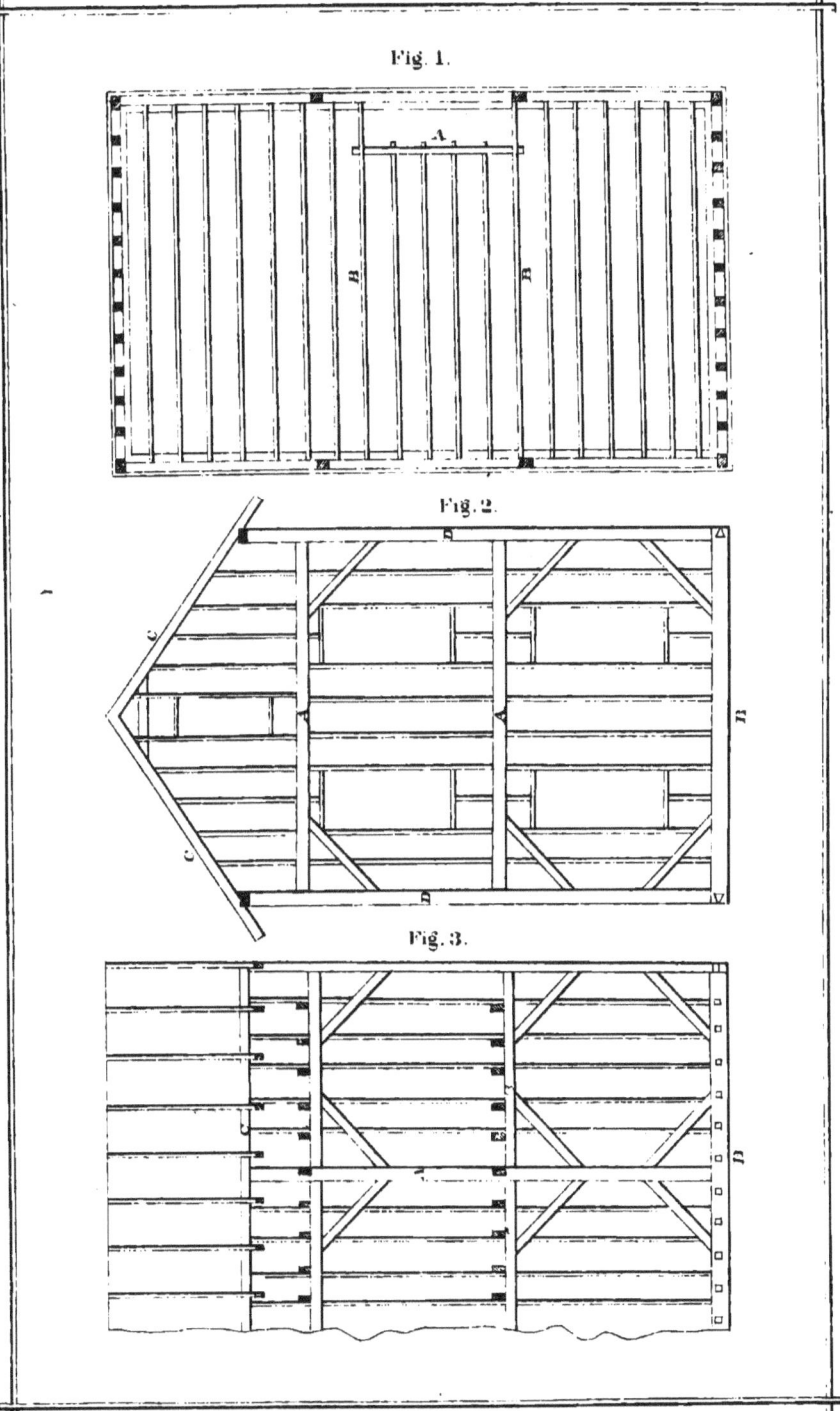

## CONSTRUCTION OF ROOFS.

In old Gothic buildings, the roof always had a high pitch, its outline formed a striking feature, and in general had a gracefull proportion with the magnitude of the building; sometimes, however, it presented a plain surface of too great extent, as the roof of Westminster Hall. Though a high roof is in perfect unison with the aspiring and pyramidal character of Gothic architecture; in the more chaste and classic style of the Greek, it is a less conspicuous object. Many of the Grecian buildings were never intended to be roofed at all; but where a roof is necessary, it was not attempted to be hidden, but constituted one of the most ornamental parts of the building. Of timber roofs, we have no examples in Grecian buildings; but the beautiful stone roof of the Octagon Tower of Andronicus Cyrrhestes, and that of the Choragic Monument of Lysicrates, are sufficient to show that they were more inclined to ornament than to hide this essential part of a building.

The height of roofs at the present time, is seldom above one-third of the span, and should never be less than one-sixth. The most usual pitch is that when the height is one-fourth of the span, or when the angle with the horizon is 26¼ degrees.

The pediments of the Greek temples make an angle of from 12 to 16 degrees with the horizon; the latter corresponds nearly with one-seventh of the span. The pediments of the Roman buildings vary from 23 to 24 degrees: 24 degrees is nearly two-ninths of the span.

## PLATE 8.

Shows the method of constructing what is termed a balloon frame. Fig. 1, shows the timber plan; Fig. 2 and 3, the front and side elevations. The foundation timbers should be of white pine; all other timbers, of spruce or eastern pine. All the tools the workman requires to construct a frame of this kind, is a saw, hammer and chisel. The side-sills should be 4x4 inches; front and rear sills four inches thick; beams 2x8, or ten inches, according to their length and the load they are required to carry. Corner post 4x4 inches; door and window joists, 3x4 inches; all other intermediate joists, 2x4 inches; plates, 4x4 inches; rafters, 3x5 inches. The two outside beams in second story, are spiked to the joists; those resting on the plates are spiked to the rafters. The enter-ties require to be 1½x4 inches let into the joists to support second story beams. Each tier of beams should have one or two courses of bridging. When the frame is completed and sheathed with one inch worked boards placed diagonally, and securely nailed to every joist, it will be quite as substantial and safe as a frame made in the usual manner.

Plate 8.

Fig. 1.

Fig. 2.

Fig. 3.

## ROOF COVERINGS.

The kinds of covering used for timber roofs, are copper, lead, iron, tinned iron, slates of different kinds, tiles, shingles. gravel, felt and cement. Taking the angle for slates to be 26½ degrees, the following table will show the degree of inclination that may be given for other materials.

| Kind of covering. | Inclination to the horizon in degrees. | | Height of roof in parts of the span. | Weight upon a square of roofing. | |
|---|---|---|---|---|---|
| | Deg. | Min. | | | |
| Tin................ | 3 | 50 | $\frac{1}{48}$ | 50 | pounds. |
| Copper,........... | 3 | 50 | $\frac{1}{48}$ | 100 | " |
| Lead,............. | 3 | 50 | $\frac{1}{48}$ | 700 | " |
| Slates, large,...... | 22 | 00 | $\frac{1}{5}$ | 1120 | " |
| "  ordinary,..... | 26 | 33 | $\frac{1}{4}$ | 900 | " |
| "  fine,......... | 26 | 33 | $\frac{1}{4}$ | 500 | " |
| Plain tiles,........ | 29 | 41 | $\frac{3}{4}$ | 1780 | " |
| Gravel............ | | | | | |
| Felt and Cement.... | | | | | |

Felt and Cement or Gravel Roofing can be used at almost any inclination that other materials are used.

# FRAMING.

A knowledge of framing is the foundation of the art and science of building and should be possessed by every person professing to be a carpenter and joiner. To him who understands the different methods of finding the various cuts necessary in his work, carpentry becomes an agreeable and desirable occupation, rather than an unpleasant task, attended with anxiety and uncertainty.

The experience of workmen generally, will testify that books have, as yet, furnished them but small assistance on this subject. It is intended, therefore, to present at this time a new and complete system for finding the sections of timbers for roofs of every description by means of tangents and circles.

## PLATE 9.

*Exhibits a new and easy system of lines for finding the lengths of rafters; the backing of the hips and the lines for cutting the jack-rafters and purlins, for right, acute and obtuse angled building, where the pitches are the same, or of different inclinations.*

Let A B C D be the plan of the roof A E D, and B F C the plan of the hips, A G D the pitch of the roof and G H the height of the roof; then A G and G D will be the length of the common rafters; make K L equal to the length of the common rafters, join B L, which gives you the length of the hip-rafter. Divide K L into as many parts as you have jack-rafters, and from the points of division, draw the dotted lines parallel to K B, and from the points of intersection with the line B L, draw the jack-rafters 1 1, 2 2, etc. The bevel for

Plate 9.

Fig. 1.

the face of the jack-rafters and hips is shown at M; the down bevel for the jack-rafters, is shown at G; the down bevel for the hips is shown at N.

To obtain the backing of the hip-rafter. At any point on the line A H, with one point of the compass, describe the arc to touch the common rafter; then A C becomes a tangent to the circle P R; draw the line O S at right-angles to A E; from the point S, draw the line S T tangential to the circle P R; join O V, then S V O is a section of the roof, cut perpendicular to the hip-rafter and through the line S O, and consequently S V O will be the angle to bevel the hips required.

To find the mitre or butt-joints of the purlin against the hip-rafters, make the line 1, 2, Fig. 1, the pitch of the roof; take any point 3 and describe the circles, 1, 4 and 5, 6; then from the points of intersection with the line 4, 3, draw the lines 4, 7 and 6, 8 parallel to C D; join 8, 9 and 7, 9, then the bevel shown at 7 will give the down cut on the side 5, 3, and the bevel shown at 8 will give the face cut of the purlin shown on the line 1, 3.

# CARPENTRY.

### PLATE 10.

Exhibits the application of the foregoing principles to obtuse and acute angles. The same process is observed as in Plate 9. The down bevel shown at 10, gives the down cut for the common and jack-rafters; the bevels shown at 1 and 2 are the face bevels for the jack and hip-rafters. Those shown at 3 and 4 are the down bevels for the hip-rafters; the bevels shown at 6, 6, are for the face of the purlin and applied to the line 7, 8; those shown at 5, 5 are applied on the line 9, 7.

Plate 10.

CARPENTRY. 25

## A PRACTICAL METHOD

OF FINDING THE NUMBER OF CUBIC FEET AND INCHES CONTAINED IN TIMBER AND OTHER METERIALS.

If the length be given in feet and inches, and the section, or end, in inches, multiply the sides of the section by each other, and divide by twelve. Also divide the length by 12; multiply these two dimensions by each other duodecimally, and the product will be the contents in cubic feet and inches.

*Example.*—Find the number of cubic feet, in a piece of timber 28 feet long, 11 inches wide, and 3 inches thick.

```
                                   ft.
   in.                          12)28 the length,
   11 ⎫                            ─────
    3 ⎬ the sides.   Multiply     2·4
      ⎭                  by       2·9
   ─────                          ─────
   12)33                          4·8
   ─────                          1·9·0
    2·9                           ─────
                                  6·5 gives 6 ft. 5 in.
                                          the solidity.
```

*Example 2.*—Find the cubic contents of 4 quarters or studs, each 12 feet 6 inches long, and 6 inches wide, by 2½ inches thick.

```
   2½ ⎫                      12·6 the length
    6 ⎬ the sides.              4 the number of pieces
      ⎭                      ─────
   ─────                     12)50·0
   12)15                     ─────
   ─────                      4·2
    1·3            Multiply   1·3
                      by     ─────
                              4·2
                              1·0·6
                             ─────
                              5·2·6 gives 5 ft. 2 in. and
                                    6 parts the solidity.
```

4

## PLATE 11.

*Shows the method of framing a roof with a transept on one side, where the intersections of the roofs form internal angles on one side of the plan; also the plan of the gable standing in the line of the side opposite the transept.*

Let A B C D E F G H be the plan of the roof, G E and B F, the plan of the angle rafters, B I and B J the length of the common rafters. Divide the rafters G I and G R into as many parts as you require jack-rafters, as shown at Fig. 1 and Fig. 3; drop the lines from I and J, to N and O; join N G and N F, also O G and O B, then the bevel shown at O, will be the face bevel for the jack-rafters, shown at Fig. 1, and the bevel shown at N will be the face bevel for the jack-rafters shown at Fig. 3; the bevel shown at N and O gives the lines for mitreing the face of the hip-rafters; the down bevels for the jack-rafters are shown at I and J, and the down bevel for the hip-rafters is shown at P. To find the backing for the valley shown at B, draw the line L M at right-angles to B F; then with one point of the compass in the points L and M, describe the circles touching the lines B J and B I; then from the points L and M, draw the tangential lines M S and L S, the internal angle thus found will be the angle to bevel the valley-rafter. The external angle shown on the opposite side of the tangential lines would be the backing for a hip-rafter, where different pitches of the roof intersect each other. The method of finding the backing for the angle-rafter to support the gable-rafters shown at Fig. 1, is the same as shown on Plates 9 and 10, and consequently needs no explanation.

FIGURE 1.—Shows an elevation of the gable with the pitch of the main roof, shown at G T and E S. The object is to

Plate 11.

show the workman that the cuts for the jack-rafters may be found from the pitches of the roofs when they are known without reference to the plan; the bevels here shown are the same as those shown at O and N.

FIGURE 4.—Shows how to erect a perpendicular from the extremity of a given line. Let A B be the given straight line and B the point from which to erect the perpendicular. Take any point C with C B as radius and describe the circle D B E, produce the line D C to E, join E B and the line thus obtained will be the required perpendicular.

## PLATE 12.

FIGURE 1.—Exhibits the method of finding the backing of the hip-rafters, the lengths and cuts of jack-rafters, where the pitches are not at the same angle of elevation. Let A B C and D, be the plan of the roof, A E B the plan of the hips, F G and J H the height of the rafters; join A G and A H, then A G will be the pitch of the roof over the line E J, and A H will be the pitch over the line E F, and E A will be the line of intersection. The down and face bevels for the jack-rafters and hips are all shown; the principle and method of finding the section of the hip is the same as shown on Plate 9.

FIGURE 2.—Exhibits a method of finding the distance to kerf the back string for a circular stairs so that when secured in its place the saw-kerfs shall be closed. To find the distance the saw-kerfs shall be from each other, make C D equal the radius of the required circle shown at A B, then take a piece the thickness of the string-piece, any width; make a saw-kerf in the centre as shown at C, secure the piece at C and F, move the piece from D until the saw-kerf is closed at C, which will give the points for the saw-kerfs required, as shown on the curve line at E and D.

FIGURE 3.—Exhibits a very cheap and expeditious plan for framing a roof to span from forty to seventy feet. It requires no explanation, further than to say that the tie need not be more than 5x8 inches; the rafters and braces 5x5 inches; the battens of one inch boards spiked to the timbers with large nails. It is believed to be the best roof than can be constructed, as it has all the advantages of a solid mass without the great weight and the disadvantages of the shrinkage of material which is almost entirely obviated by the crossing of the fibres of the wood.

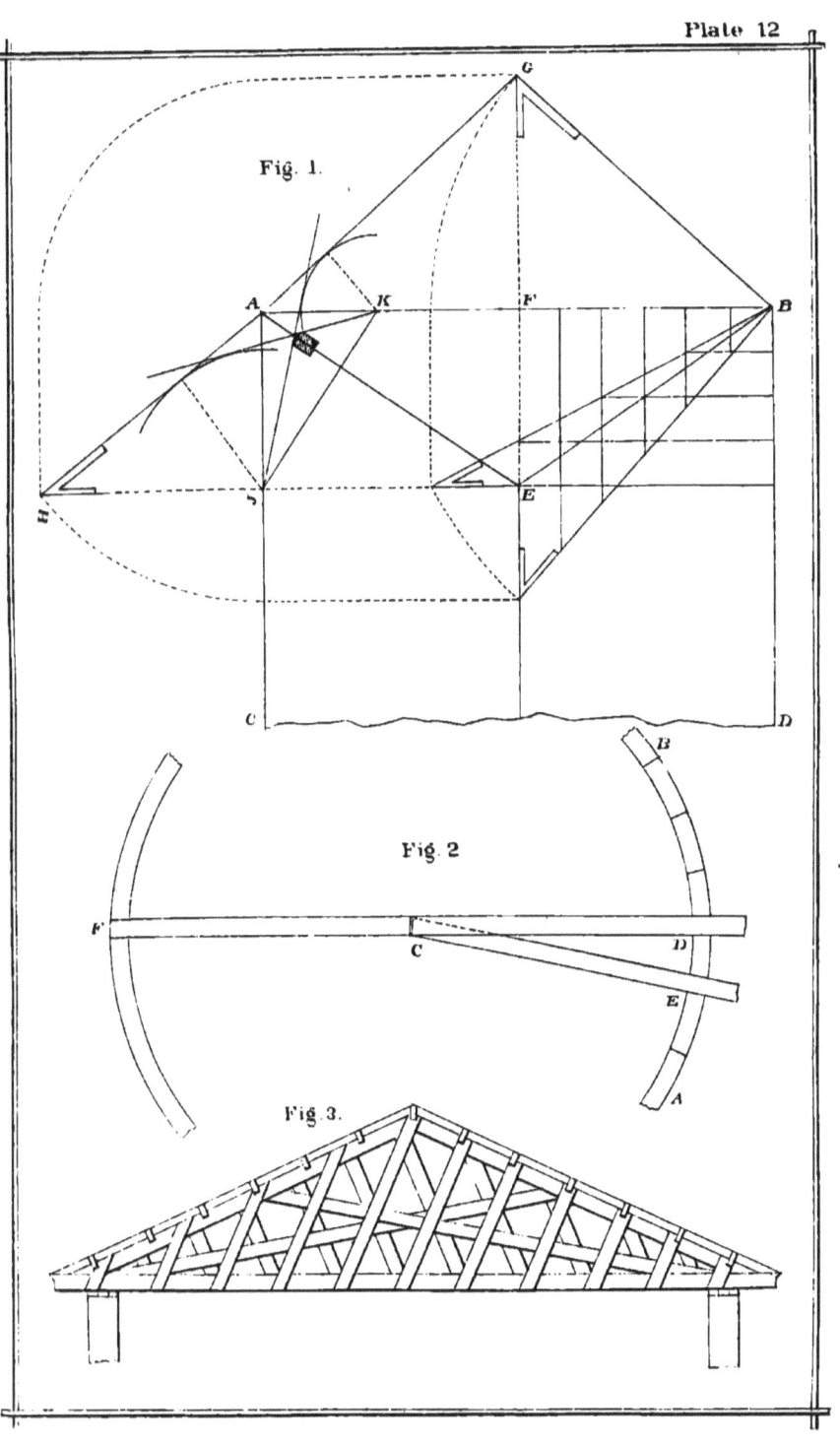

Plate 12

Fig. 1.

Fig. 2

Fig. 3.

CARPENTRY. 29

## A PRACTICAL METHOD

To find the superficial contents of boards and timber. For boards multiply the width in inches by the length in feet and divide by 12.

*Example.*—Find the number of feet in a board 1 inch thick 9 inches wide and 13 feet long.

$$\begin{array}{r} 13 \\ 9 \\ \hline 12\overline{)117} \\ \hline 9\cdot 9 = 9 \text{ feet 9 inches.} \end{array}$$

*Example.*—2nd, find the number of feet in a piece of timber 3x10 inches 21 feet long.

```
        10 inches long.
         3   "   thick.
        ───
     12)30
        2·6 inches in each foot in length.
        21 feet long.
        ───
        42
        10·6
        ───
        52·6 Gives 52 feet 6 inches, the number
                of feet in the piece.
```

## PLATE 13.

Exhibits the method of framing an obtuse and acute-angled building, the plan being a rhomboid, where the projection of the rafters are supported by braces. The lines for finding the shoulders for braces to fit the obtuse and acute-angles; also the section or backing of rafters, and the bevel required to cut the rafters so that their ends shall be in the plane of the building.

Let A (Fig. 1), be the plan of the post, B the plan of the rafter, C the elevation of the post, and D the plate, Fig. 2, and 3 the braces, E the elevation of the rafters. To find the shoulders of the braces, draw F G parallel to the edge of the post; make H, the under side of the brace, equal in width to B, Fig. 1; then at the intersection of the lower line of the brace with the line of the post, place one point of the compass and describe the arc shown at G; draw the tangential line at right-angles to the line of the brace, and from the point of intersection, draw the bevel line to the line of the post; then the bevel shown at H will give the lines for the edges of the braces shown at Fig. 2 and 3. Fig. 4 is an elevation of the rafter. The method of finding the bevel at the edge of the rafter so that it shall be in the plane of the roof, is shown at E. The bevel for the butt-joints at the apex or peak of the roof is shown at F.

Figure 5.—To draw a line making equal angles with two given converging lines. Let A D and B C be two converging lines; draw G H parallel to C B, and I H parallel to D A; make G H and H I equal; from the points G and I, describe the arcs J K, and through the points of intersection J and K, draw the line E F which will be at equal angles with the lines A D and C B.

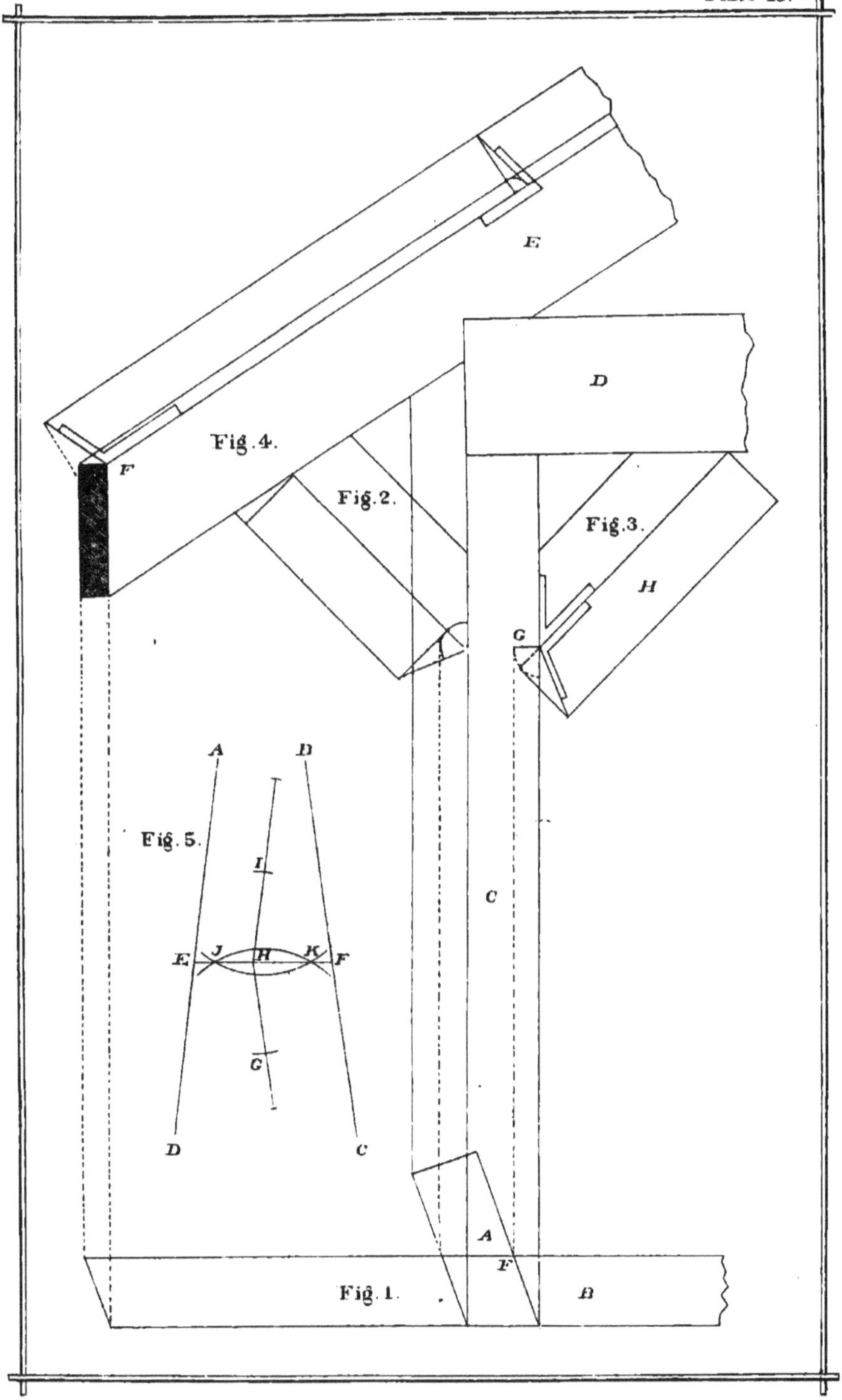

Plate 13.

Fig. 4.
Fig. 2.
Fig. 3.
Fig. 5.
Fig. 1.

CARPENTRY. 31

## LONG MEASURE.

Long measure is used in measuring length or distance only, without regard to breadth or depth. Its denominations are *leagues, miles, furlongs, rods, yards feet and inches.*

| | | |
|---|---|---|
| 12 inches | make | 1 foot. |
| 3 feet | " | 1 yard. |
| 5½ yards or 16½ feet | " | 1 rod. |
| 40 rods | " | 1 furlong. |
| 8 furlongs or 320 rods | " | 1 mile. |
| 3 miles | " | 1 league. |

NOTE.—4 inches make 1 hand; 9 inches 1 span; 18 inches 1 cubit; 6 feet 1 fathom; 4 rods or 100 links 1 chain; 25 links 1 rod; $7\frac{92}{100}$ inches 1 link.

The chain is commonly used in measuring roads and land, and is called Gunter's chain, from the name of the inventor.

A knot, in sea phrase, answers to a nautical or geographical mile of 5280 feet.

Mariner's measure is a kind of long measure used in estimating distances at sea.

| | | |
|---|---|---|
| 6 feet | make | 1 fathom |
| 120 fathoms | " | 1 cable-length. |
| 880 fathoms or 7½ cable | " | 1 mile. |

## PLATE 14.

FIGURE 1.—*Shows the method of finding the cuts in a mitre-box by which to cut a sprung moulding when a bevel cannot be applied.*—Let A be the moulding in position C, D the mitre given to find the bevels to cut the mitre-box. With one point of the compass in E, describe the semicircle F G H; drop the lines from F G I H to K C D J, at right-angles to F H; draw D J and C K parallel to F H; join J L and L K, then in the angles E L J and E L K, will be found the bevels required to cut the mitre-box. The bevel shown at M will be applied to the top, and the bevel shown at N will be applied to the side of the box.

FIGURE 2.—*Shows the plan and elevation of an octagonal roof, to find the angle and jack-rafters.*—On the plan produce the lines B A and C D to the line E F; join E G and F G, then E G F will be the elevation of the roof. To find the backing of the angle-rafters. With one point of the compass at H describe the arc, touching the pitch line of the roof as shown; from the point B draw the line B I, making the line thus drawn a tangent to the circle, and from the point of intersection with the line A C, draw the line to H, then in the angle thus found will be seen the angle to bevel the angle-rafters as shown at J. To find the lengths and cuts of the angle and jack-rafters, draw K L perpendicular to D C, and equal to F G; join C L and D L, then the bevel shown at N will be for the face of the angle-rafters at their intersection, and for the face of the jack-rafters, the down bevel for jack-rafters is shown at G; the down bevel for the angle-rafters is found by making C M equal one-half of A C, and L M equal P G, then at O will be seen the down bevel for the angle-rafter.

FIGURE 3.—Shows the application of the same principle to the framing of a roof over a polygonal plan of six sides and does not require any explanation.

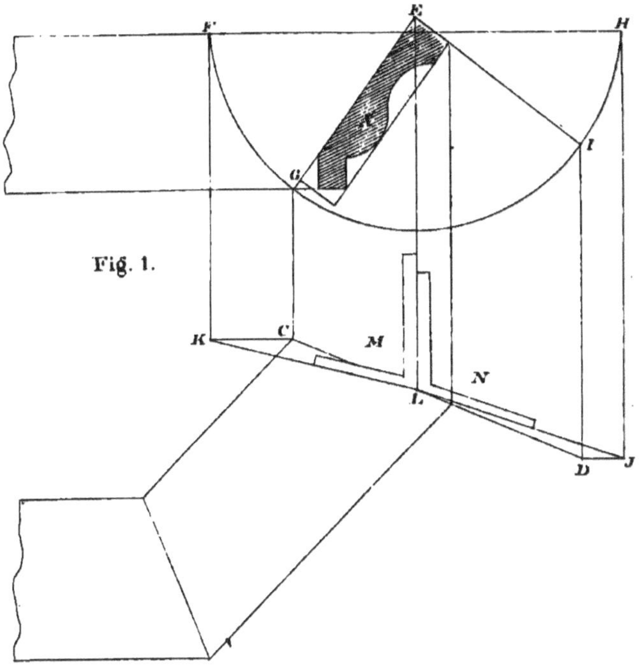

Plate 14.

Fig. 1.

Fig. 2.

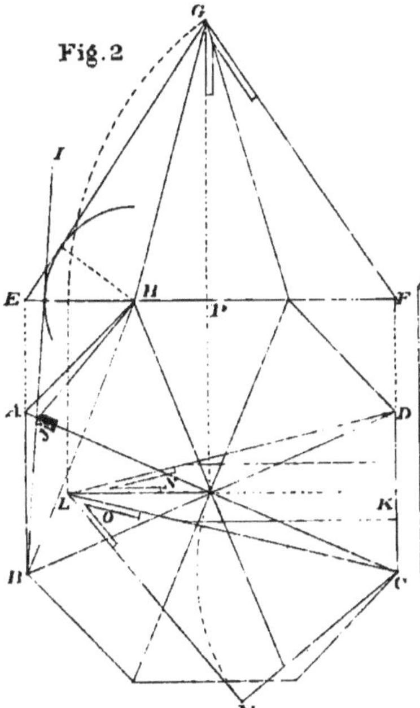

Fig. 3.

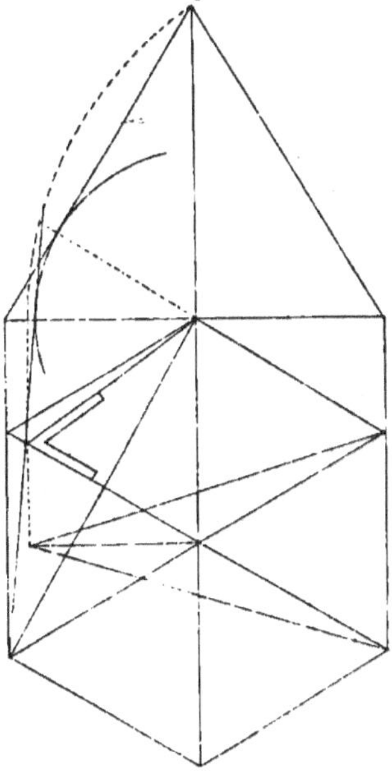

## PLATE 15.

*Exhibits plans and elevations of octagonal and square spires for churches or bell-towers, as shown at Fig. 1 and 2.* To find the lines for the face of the timbers, make the dotted line A B shown on the plan, Fig. 1, equal C D on the elevation; join E A and F A, then the bevel shown at G will give the lines for the face of the enter-ties; and the bevel shown at H will give the lines for the upper and lower sides; the bevel for cutting the angular timbers to intersect each other as shown at D will be found at A. The methods of finding the backing of the angular timbers is precisely the same as shown on Plate 9.

FIGURE 2.—Shows the application of the same principles to the framing of a square spire or bell-tower; a bare inspection of the Figure is sufficient for its comprehension.

FIGURE 3.—*Through any three points to describe the circumference of a circle, or when the centre of a circle is lost, to find it.*—Let A B C be the three given points; join A B and C B, and from the points A B C as centres, describe the arcs E F and D G; through the points of intersection draw the lines E F and D G, produce them until they meet, which will be the point or centre from which to describe the circle which shall touch the points, A B C.

FIGURE 4.—*To erect a perpendicular to a given line from a point in the same.* From the point C take any two equal distances, as C B and C A, and from the points A B as centres, describe two arcs intersecting each other as at D; join D and C and the line thus obtained will be the required perpendicular.

Plate 15.

## WEIGHT OR FORCE.

REQUIRED TO TEAR ASUNDER ONE SQUARE INCH OF THE DIFFERENT MATERIALS USED IN THE CONSTRUCTION OF BUILDINGS.

### WOODS AND METALS.

| | | | |
|---|---|---|---|
| Oak, American, | 17,300 | Swedish Iron, | 78,850 |
| Oak, English, | 19,800 | English Iron, | 55,772 |
| Beach, | 17,700 | French Iron, | 61,041 |
| Ash, | 16,700 | Russian Iron, | 59,472 |
| Elm, | 13,489 | Cast Iron, | 42,000 |
| Walnut, | 8,130 | Steel, Soft, | 120,000 |
| Norway Pine, | 14,300 | Ivory, | 16,000 |
| Georgia Pine, | 7,818 | Marble, | 8,700 |
| White Pine, | 8,800 | Whalebone, | 7,600 |
| Iron Wire, | 113,077 | | |

*To find the strength of Cohesion.* Multiply area of section in inches by the weight required to tear one inch asunder, and the product is the strength in pounds.

## WEIGHTS

REQUIRED TO CRUSH ONE CUBIC INCH OF SEVERAL MATERIALS USED IN THE CONSTRUCTION OF BUILDINGS.

| METALS. | | WOODS. | |
|---|---|---|---|
| Cast Iron, | 116,700 | Elm, | 1,284 |
| Brass, | 154,784 | American Pine, | 1,606 |
| Copper, Cast, | 116,102 | White Deal, | 1,928 |
| Lead, Cast, | 8,042 | White Oak, | 3,240 |
| | | English Oak, | 3,860 |

### STONES.

| | | | |
|---|---|---|---|
| Freestone, | 18,000 | Brick, hard, | 1,754 |
| Limestone, Black, | 19,450 | Brick, soft, | 1,224 |
| Granite, Blue, | 20,890 | Chalk, | 1,040 |

## PLATE 16.

FIGURE 1.—*Shows the method of finding the raking mould to any angle of elevation, also for a given elevation to any angle inclining towards a straight line.*

Divide the surface of the horizontal moulding, here shown, into any number of parts, and from the points thus obtained, draw the inclining parallel lines to the required angle of elevation; from the same points draw vertical lines to meet the horizontal line A B, and, with one point of the compass on A, transfer the points between A and B, on the horizontal line, to the inclining line; perpendicular to the inclining line, draw the corresponding lines to meet the parallels, and through the points of intersection trace the raking moulding required.

FIGURE 2.—*Shows the method of finding the raking moulding to any angle inclining towards a straight line.*

To find the raking mould when the gable is placed over any of the diverging lines shown on the plan. Let B A C be a right angle, A H C a straight line, and A D B the elevation of the roof. Divide the circle F H into any number of parts, make the line F G equal to the development or stretch-out of the circle; produce the lines B F A and G H until they intersect each other, and at their intersection will be the point from which to draw the radiating lines, 1 1 2 2, etc.; join G B, then parallel to G B, draw the lines from the points 1 2, etc., to the line F B, and from the line F B parallel to the line B D, to intersect the line D F, then the lines from A to the line F D will give the elevation to draw the raking-moulding for any of the diverging lines shown on the plan; the line A 1, on the elevation, will be the pitch to draw the raking-mould standing on the line A J on the plan, and the line A 5, would be the pitch to draw

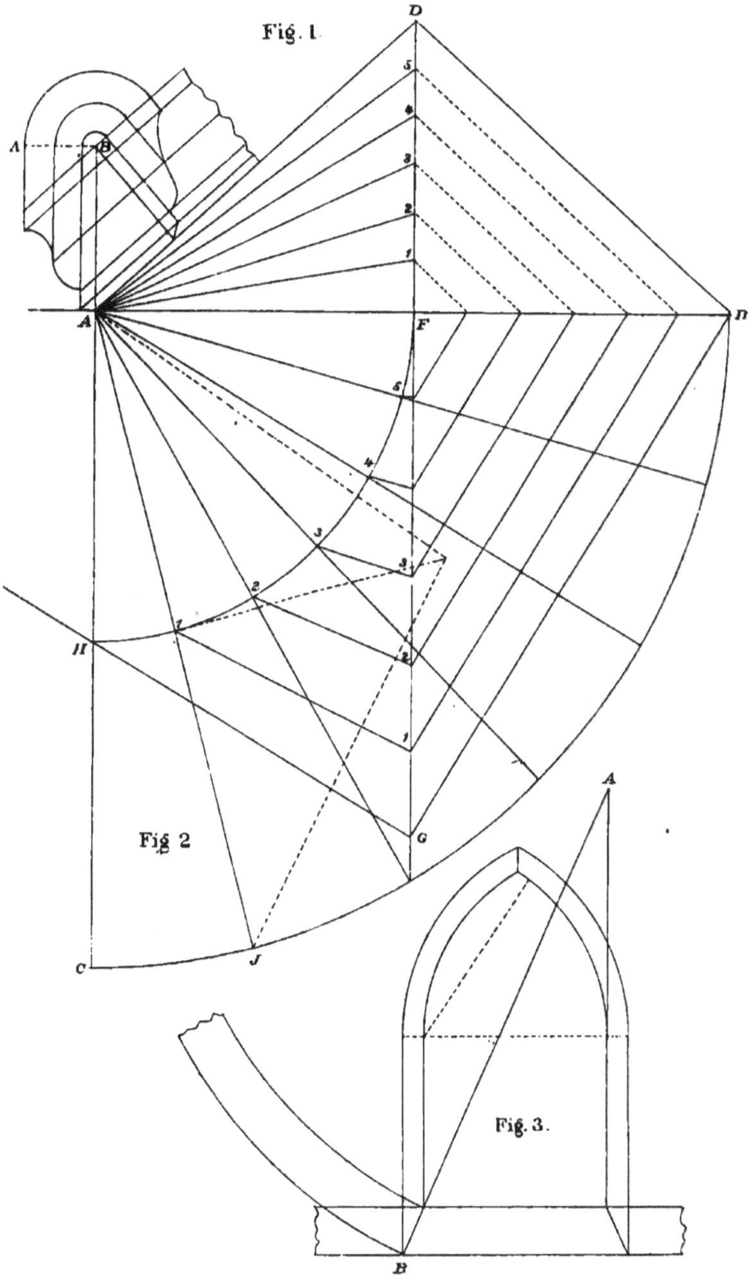

Plate 16.

Fig. 1.

Fig 2

Fig. 3.

# SPLAYED WORK.

## PLATE 17.

FIGURES 1, 2 AND 3.—*Shows the method of finding the lines for the face and edges of a piece set to a given angle, oblique to the base, to mitre over acute, obtuse, or right-angles.*

FIGURE 1.—Let A B C be the plan of an acute-angle, B D the line of intersection, and E the piece placed oblique to the base. To find the line for the face of the piece, place one point of the compass at I, and describe the arc A C; draw the tangential line G H parallel to A B; join B D and H D, then in the angle G H D will be found the bevel for the face of the piece E. To find the line to cut the edge, place one point of the compass at I, and describe the arc J K; draw the tangential line K L parallel to A B, join L D; then in the angle K L D will be found the bevel for the edge of the piece E,

The Plate will be found very useful to workman, in constructing boxes where the sides are required to be placed oblique to the vase.

FIGURES 2 AND 3.—Exhibits the application of the same principle to an obtuse and right-angle, and a bare inspection of the Figure will show that the process is precisely the same as shown at Fig. 1.

FIGURE 4.—Represents a method of finding the lines for a butt-joint when required, instead of a mitre and is the same principle shown at Plate 9, for finding the backing of a hip-rafter.

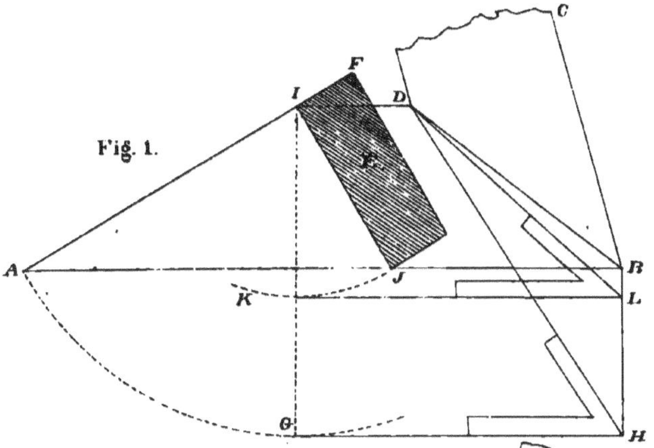

Plate 17

Fig. 1.

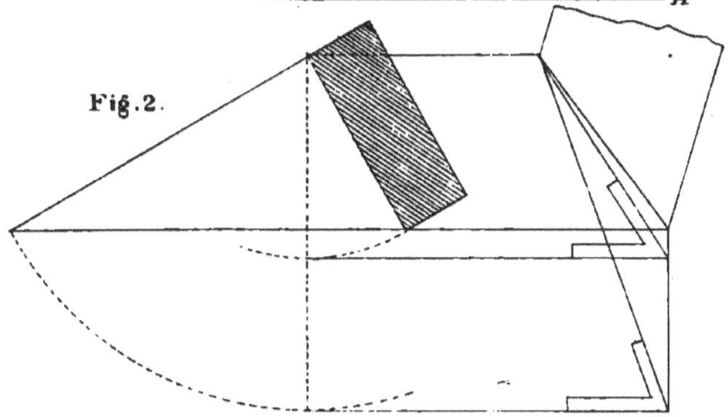

Fig. 2.

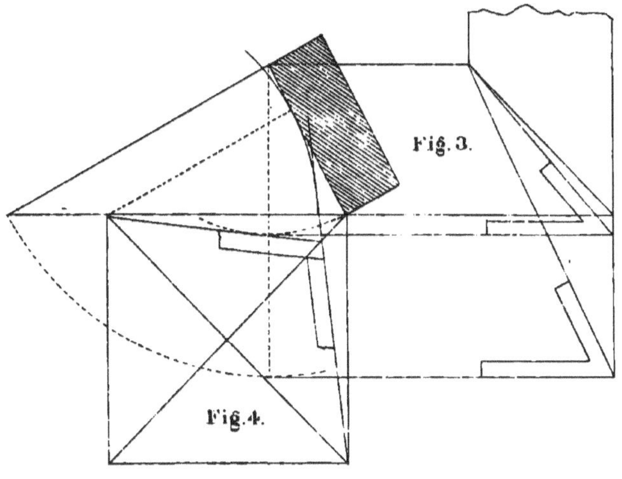

Fig. 3.

Fig. 4.

## OF POSTS.

According to the experiments of Rondelet, when the height of a square post is less than about seven or eight times the side of its base, it cannot be bent by any pressure less than that which would crush it. The internal mechanism of the resisting forces, when timber yields by crushing, is not exactly understood. In timber the resistance to crushing is less than the cohesive force. The resistance of timber to crushing appears to increase in a higher ratio than that of the area of its section.

The load a piece of timber will bear, when pressed in the direction of its length, without risk of being crushed, may be found by the following rule:

Multiply the area of the piece of timber, in inches, by the weight that is capable of crushing a square inch of the same kind of wood, then, one-fourth of the product will give the load in pounds that the piece would bear with safety.

If the area that would support a given weight be required, divide four times the weight by the number of pounds that would crush a square inch, and the quotient is the area in inches.

The length should never exceed ten times the side of the section to give the above results; for when the length is greater than about ten times the thickness, the piece will bend before it crushes.

40     SPLAYED WORK.

## PLATE 18.

FIGURE 1.—Exhibits an elevation of a box whose sides are of different inclinations. Figure 2, the plan of the box E F, and D C H the lines of the mitres. The bevels for the sides are shown at 1, 2 and 3. Those for the edges at Figures 4, 5 and 6. Further explanations are omitted, believing that the workman, after an inspection of the Figures, will be able to construct any thing of the kind when required.

FIGURES 3 AND 4.—*Shows the method of finding the lines for mitreing together a grain-mill hopper; also to find the angle-pieces that are required to secure the pieces together at their intersections.*—Let A B C D, Fig 4, be the plan of the angular box, and Fig. 3 the elevation, with one point of the compass on E, describe the dotted curve to intersect the line B C in F; draw the tangential line F G parallel to D C; produce A D to G, join I H and I F, then I H F will be the form and size of one side of the grain-mill hopper required; and as it is usual to place the sides at an angle of 45°, in this case, the same bevel shown at F for the sides will answer for the edges. The method shown on the plan for finding the angle-piece, also shows a butt-joint and are obtained in the same manner as described for finding the backing of hip-rafters on Plate 9.

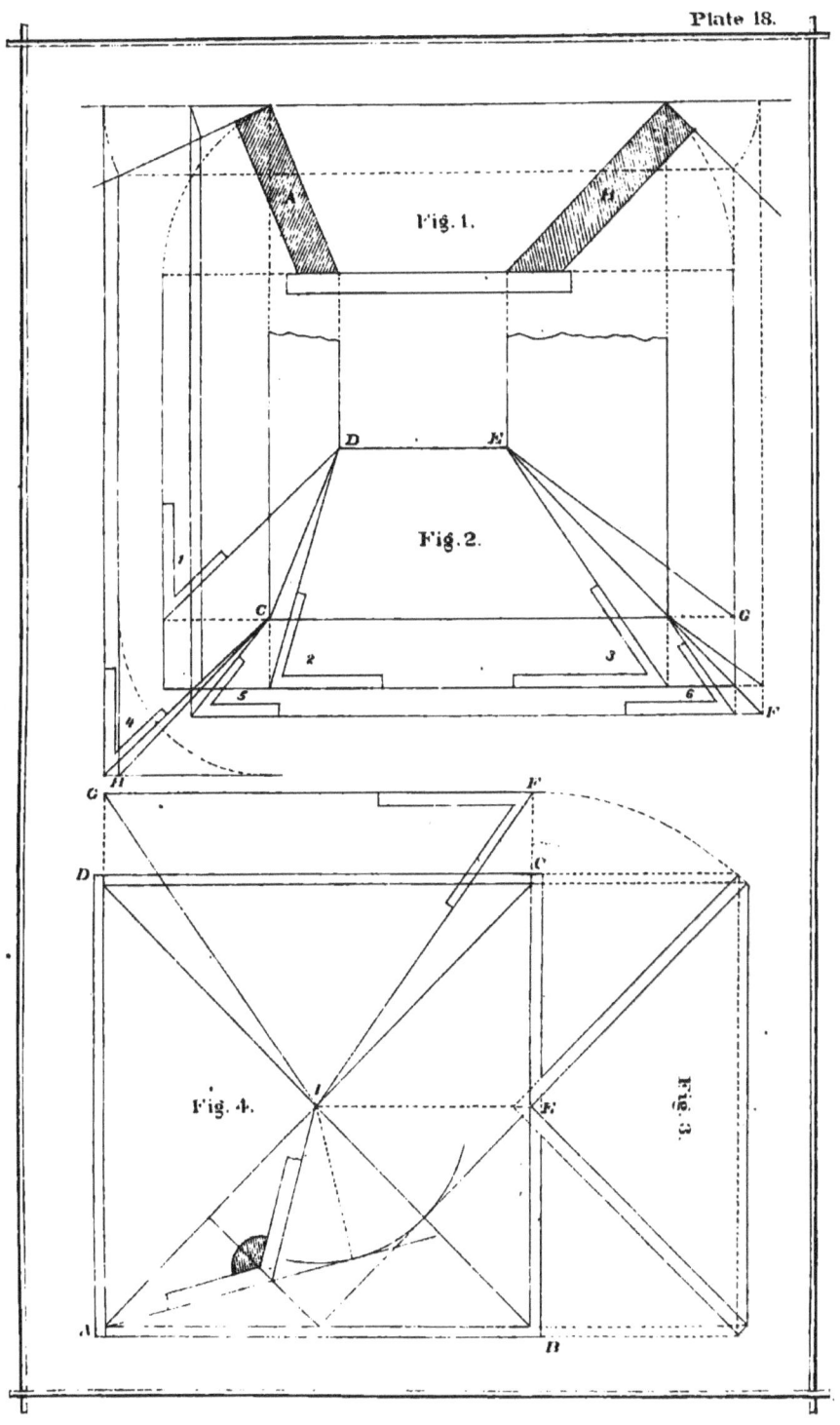

## WEIGHT IN POUNDS

OF CUBIC FOOT OF WOOD AND STONE.

| WOOD. | | STONE. | |
|---|---|---|---|
| Apple-tree, | 49.6 | Flint, | 163.2 |
| Ash, | 52.9 | Blue Granite, | 164.1 |
| Birch, | 33.2 | Lime Stone, | 199. |
| American Cedar, | 35.1 | Grindstone, | 134. |
| Elm, | 42. | Slate Stone, | 167. |
| White Pine, | 35.6 | Marble, | 170. |
| Yellow Pine, | 41.1 | Free Stone, | 150. |
| Mahogany, | 66.5 | African Marble, | 169.2 |
| Maple, | 47. | Egyptian Marble, | 166.8 |
| Mulberry, | 56.1 | Italian Marble, | 166.1 |
| Oak, | 58-74 | Roman Marble, | 172.2 |
| Live Oak, | 70. | | |

OTHER SUBSTANCES.

| | | | |
|---|---|---|---|
| Cast Iron, | 450.55 | Air, | .07529 |
| Wrought Iron, | 486.65 | Steam, | .03689 |
| Steel, | 489.8 | Loose Earth or Sand, | 95. |
| Copper, | 555. | Common Soil, | 124. |
| Lead, | 708.75 | Strong Soil, | 127. |
| Brass, | 537.75 | Clay, | 135. |
| Tin, | 456. | Clay and Stones, | 160. |
| Salt Water, (Sea,) | 64.3 | Cork, | 15. |
| Fresh Water, | 62.5 | Brick, | 125. |
| | | Tallow, | 59. |

## PLATE 19.

*Exhibits a method of constructing a circular desk; also a plan and elevation of a circular seat.*—Fig. 1 shows the elevation. Fig. 2 the plan of the circular desk. Produce the lines A H and F H indefinitely, draw the line H J, the inclination of the desk. With one point of the compass in H describe the dotted line from L and produce the same to K P; then with K P for radius, and one point of the compass in K, describe the curve line P F. At right-angles to H J, draw the line F B tangential to the curve P F, then B F gives the radius to describe the rib standing over the chord line A E on the plan. The same method is used for finding the radius for the rib over the chord line C D. If any more ribs are required, produce the lines H E and H A, and at the intersection of the chord line, draw the radius parallel to the line E I, and where it intersects the line F G, will be the point to place one point of the compass to describe the rib.

FIGURE 3.—Shows the side of the piece to be bent to form the inclining circular front. The radius to describe the circles are taken from the line H J, as shown on the plan. The radiated lines shown on the piece, exhibits the method of grooving for the keys required to shape the piece.

FIGURES 4 AND 5.—Shows the plan and elevation of a circular seat, with an inclining back, and the method of finding the curved pieces bent around and forming a continuous back to a circular seat in such a manner that the edges shall be parallel to the plane of the seat. In explanation, it is simply necessary to say that the principle is the same as that applied to finding a veneer for a Gothic-head jamb, splayed alike all around.

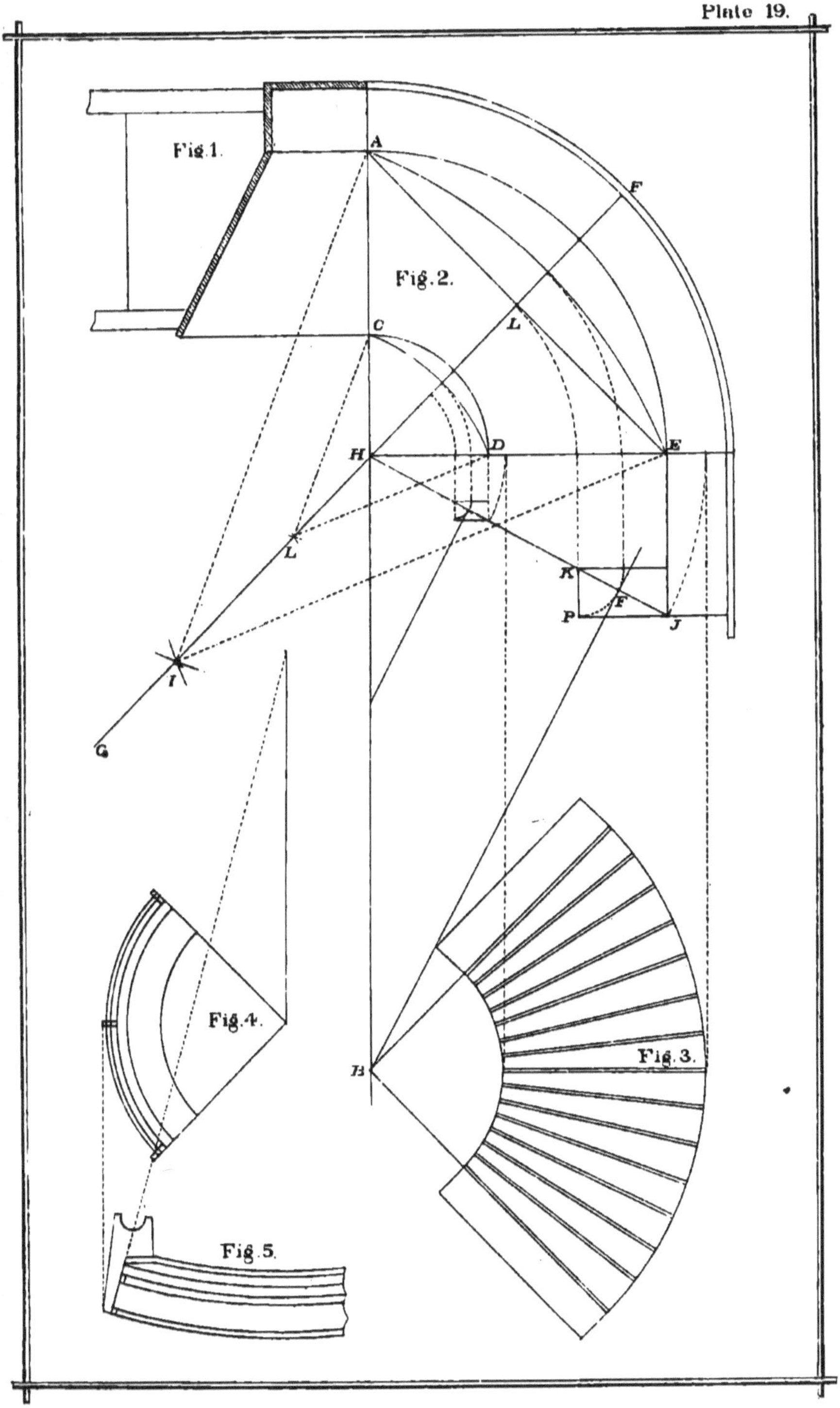

Plate 19.

Fig. 1.
Fig. 2.
Fig. 3.
Fig. 4.
Fig. 5.

## ADHESION OF NAILS.

Every carpenter is familiar with the use of the nail, and possesses a practical knowledge, more or less accurate, of the force of adhesion of different nails, and in different substances, so as to decide, without difficulty, what number, and of what length, may be sufficient to fasten together substances of various shapes, and subject to various strains. But interesting as this subject unquestionably is, it has not been till very recently that the necessary experiments have been made to determine, 1st, the adhesive force of different nails when driven into wood of different species, 2d, the actual weight, without impulse, necessary to force a nail a given depth; and 3d, the force required to extract the nail when so driven. The obtaining of this useful knowledge was reserved for Mr. B. Bevan, a gentleman well known in the mechanical and scientific world for the accuracy with which his experiments are conducted.

Mr. Bevan observes, that the theoretical investigation points out an equality of resistance to the entrance and extraction of a nail, supposing the thickness to be invariable; but as the general shape of nails is tapering towards the points, the resistance of entrance necesarily becomes greater than that of extraction; in some experiments he found the ratio to be about 6 to 5.

The percussive force required to drive the common sixpenny nail to the depth of one inch and a half into dry Christiana deal, with a cast iron weight of 6·275 lbs. was four blows or strokes falling freely the space of 12 inches; and the steady pressure to produce the same effect was 400 lbs.

# Mitreing Circular Mouldings.

## PLATE 20.

*Shows the method of mitreing Circular-mouldings.*—Fig. 1 and 2 shows the method of mitreing a tangential moulding into a circular moulding.

FIGURE 3.—Shows a straight moulding mitred into a circle at an angle of 45° with the line drawn through the centre of the circle.

FIGURE 4.—Shows how nearly impossible it is to perform work of this kind without the use of the compass, for describing the intersecting line.

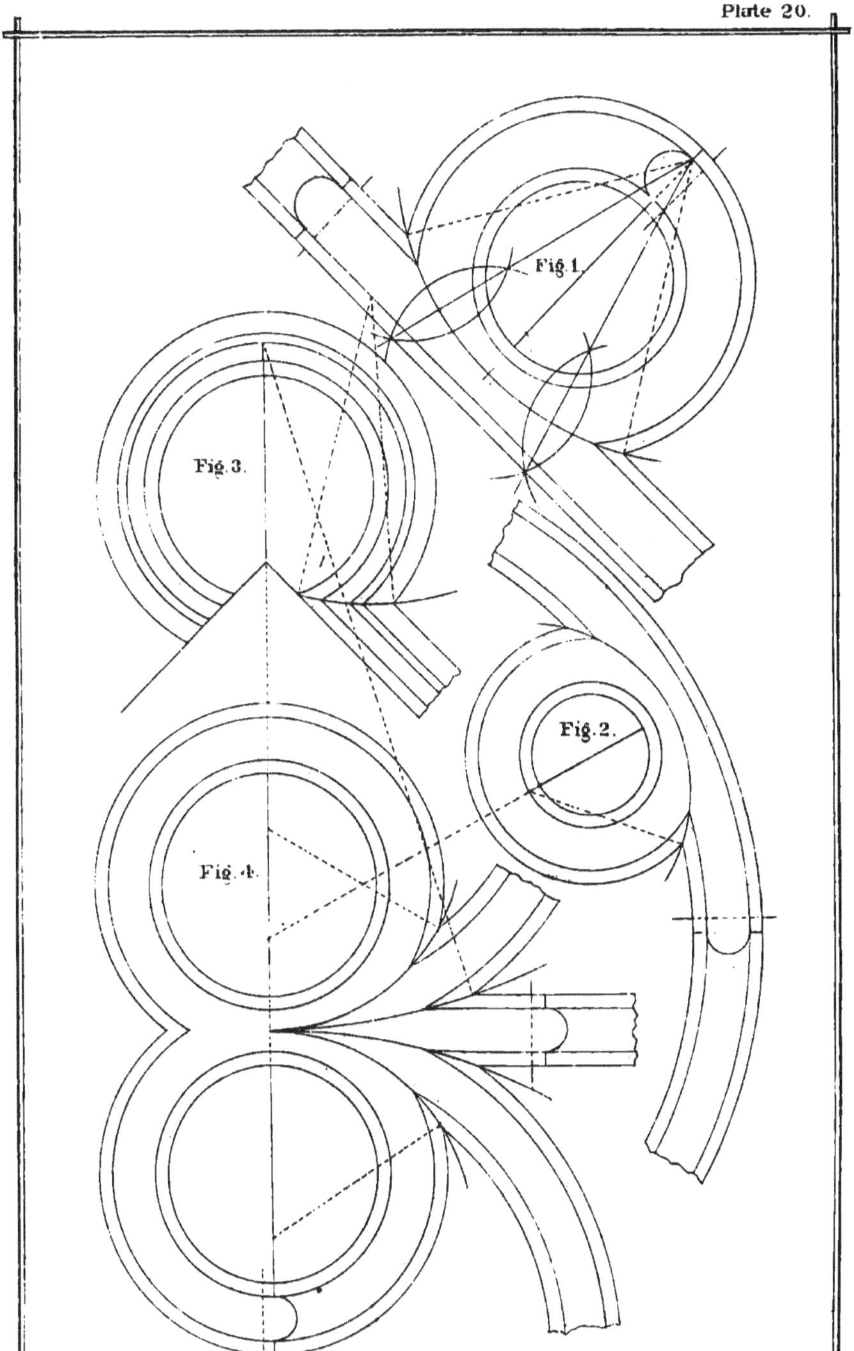

Plate 20.

Fig. 1.
Fig. 2.
Fig. 3.
Fig. 4.

## ADHESION OF NAILS.

A sixpenny nail driven into dry elm, to the depth of one inch across the grain, required a pressure of 327 pounds to extract it; and the same nail, driven endways, or longitudinally into the same wood, was extracted with a force of 257 pounds.

The same nail driven two inches endways into dry Christiana deal, was drawn by a force of 257 pounds; and to draw out one inch, under like circumstances, took 87 pounds only. The relative adhesion, therefore, in the same wood, when driven transversely and longitudinally, is 100 to 78, or about 4 to 3 in dry elm; and 100 to 46, or about 2 to 1 in deal; and in like circumstances, the relative adhesion to elm and deal is as 2 or 3 to 1.

The progressive depths of a sixpenny nail into dry Christiana deal by simple pressure were as follows:—

One quarter of an inch, a pressure of 24 lbs.
Half an inch,   ·  ·  ·    76 ——
One inch,   ·  ·  ·  ·  · 235 ——
One inch and a half,  ·  ·  · 400 ——
Two inches,  ·  ·  ·  ·  · 610 ——

In the above experiments, great care was taken by Mr. Bevan to apply the weight steadily, and towards the conclusion of each experiment, the additions did not exceed 10 lbs. at one time, with a moderative interval between, generally about one minute, sometimes 10 or 20 minutes. In other species of wood, the requisite force to extract the nail was different. Thus, to extract a common sixpenny nail from a depth of one inch out of

Dry Oak, required  ·  ·  · 507 lbs.
Dry Beech,  ·  ·  ·  ·  · 667 ——
Green Sycamore, ·  ·  ·  · 313 ——

From these experiments, we may infer that a common sixpenny nail, driven two inches into oak, would require a force of more than half a ton to extract it by a steady force.

# HAND RAILING.

The method here presented for squaring the wreath upon Geometrical principles, without the use of falling moulds for small openings, from 5 to 20 in., for straight flights and platform stairs, is the least difficult to comprehend, of any in use.

## PLATE 21.

Exhibits the elevation of a platform stairs from first to second floor. Fig. 1 shows the method of finding the point to bore for the short baluster on the second step, when you have the length of the newel and short baluster given. On the pitch-board A C B, make C A equal the difference in the lengths of the newel post and short baluster, say six inches; place the point B on the line of the centre of the newel post, and the line drawn from A will be the under side of the cap, and C A produced to the rail will give the point to bore for the first short baluster.

FIGURE 2.—Shows the plan for the hand-railing over a seven inch cylinder. The risers are placed at the point of intersection of the cylinder and string-pieces, as shown on the elevation.

FIGURE 3.—Shows the method of forming the face-mould with a cord or string, as shown on Plate 2, Fig. 1, and to be cut square through the plank.

FIGURE 4.—Exhibits the piece sawed with the bevel, shown at D, applied to the centre of the plank; then from the centre set of each side one-half of the rail which leaves a corner, to be removed from the out and inside of the piece; tack the mould on the opposite side of the corner to be removed on the out and inside of the piece, and form the wreath as shown at Fig. 5, which is an end view of the hand-rail required ready for moulding. The easing on second floor terminates one-half the height of the riser above the point to bore for the short baluster.

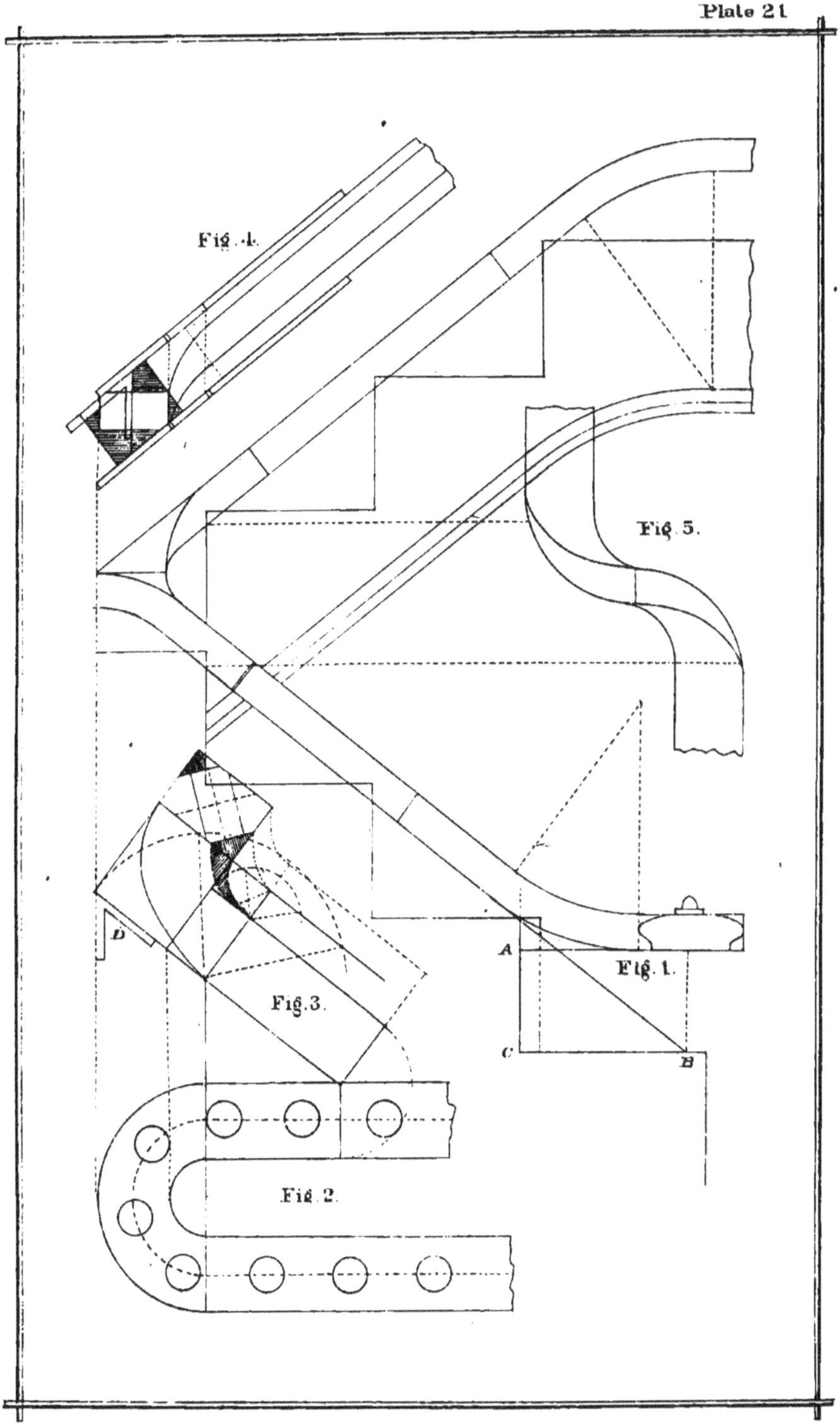

Plate 21.

Fig. 4.

Fig. 5.

Fig. 1.

Fig. 3.

Fig. 2.

## ADHESION OF SCREWS.

A common screw, of one-fifth of an inch, was found to have an adhesive force of about three times that of a sixpenny nail.

## ADHESION OF IRON PINS.

The force necessary to break or tear out a half-inch iron pin, applied in the manner of a pin to a tenon in the mortice, has likewise obtained the attention of the same celebrated experimentalist. The thickness of the board was 0.87 inch. and the distance of the centre of the hole from the end of the board 1·05 inch. The force required was 916.

As the strength of a tenon from the pin-hole may be considered in proportion to the distance from the end, and also as the thickness, we may, for this species of wood, obtain the breaking force in pounds nearly, by multiplying together one thousand times the distance of the hole from the end by the thickness of the tenon in inches.

## LENGTH OF IRON NAILS
### AND NUMBER TO A POUND.

| SIZE. | LENGTH. | NO. | SIZE. | LENGTH. | NO. |
|---|---|---|---|---|---|
| $3^d$ | $1\frac{1}{4}$ in. | 420 | $10^d$ | 3 in. | 65 |
| $4^d$ | $1\frac{1}{2}$ in. | 270 | $12^d$ | $3\frac{1}{4}$ in. | 52 |
| $5^d$ | $1\frac{3}{4}$ in. | 220 | $20^d$ | $3\frac{1}{2}$ in. | 28 |
| $6^d$ | 2 in. | 175 | $30^d$ | 4 in. | 24 |
| $8^d$ | $2\frac{1}{2}$ in. | 100 | $40^d$ | $4\frac{1}{4}$ in. | 20 |

Lead weighs 709 lbs. to cubic foot.
Water weighs $62\frac{1}{2}$ lbs. to cubic foot.

## PLATE 22.

*Exhibits a plan and elevation of a continued hand-railing from first to third floor.*—On the plan, Fig. 1, is shown the baluster placed flush with the face of the riser, from the centre will be seen the dotted line drawn parallel to the face of the riser, cutting the under side of the rail at A, then from A to B; the underside of the level-rail should be equal to half the height of the riser, or second flight. The continuation of the level-rail up the second flight is shown over the plan Fig. 2; the dotted line from the centre of baluster shows the point to bore for the first short baluster, and should be half the height of the rise, from the lower side of the level-rail. The method of finding the mould for the wreaths, is the same as shown on Plate 21.

In order to continue the same inclination around the curve and preserve the same thickness of plank for the wreath, in large openings, it is necessary to place the risers in the cylinders, as shown at Fig. 3, the plan of a twelve inch cylinder. To find the position of the risers, draw the tangential A B indefinitely, from the point B, drop the lines B D and B E, (the inclination or rake of the stairs,) above and below draw the parallel lines, showing the thickness of the rail. Now to find their position, make the line F G, equal the height of the rise and parallel to B A; produce the line F G to H, then where the line G H cuts the cylinder will be the points for the risers. Fig. 4 is an elevation of the rail E, and D represents what is termed the shank, or straight wood, and B the wreaths; the width of the rail determines the thickness of plank for the wreath and easings.

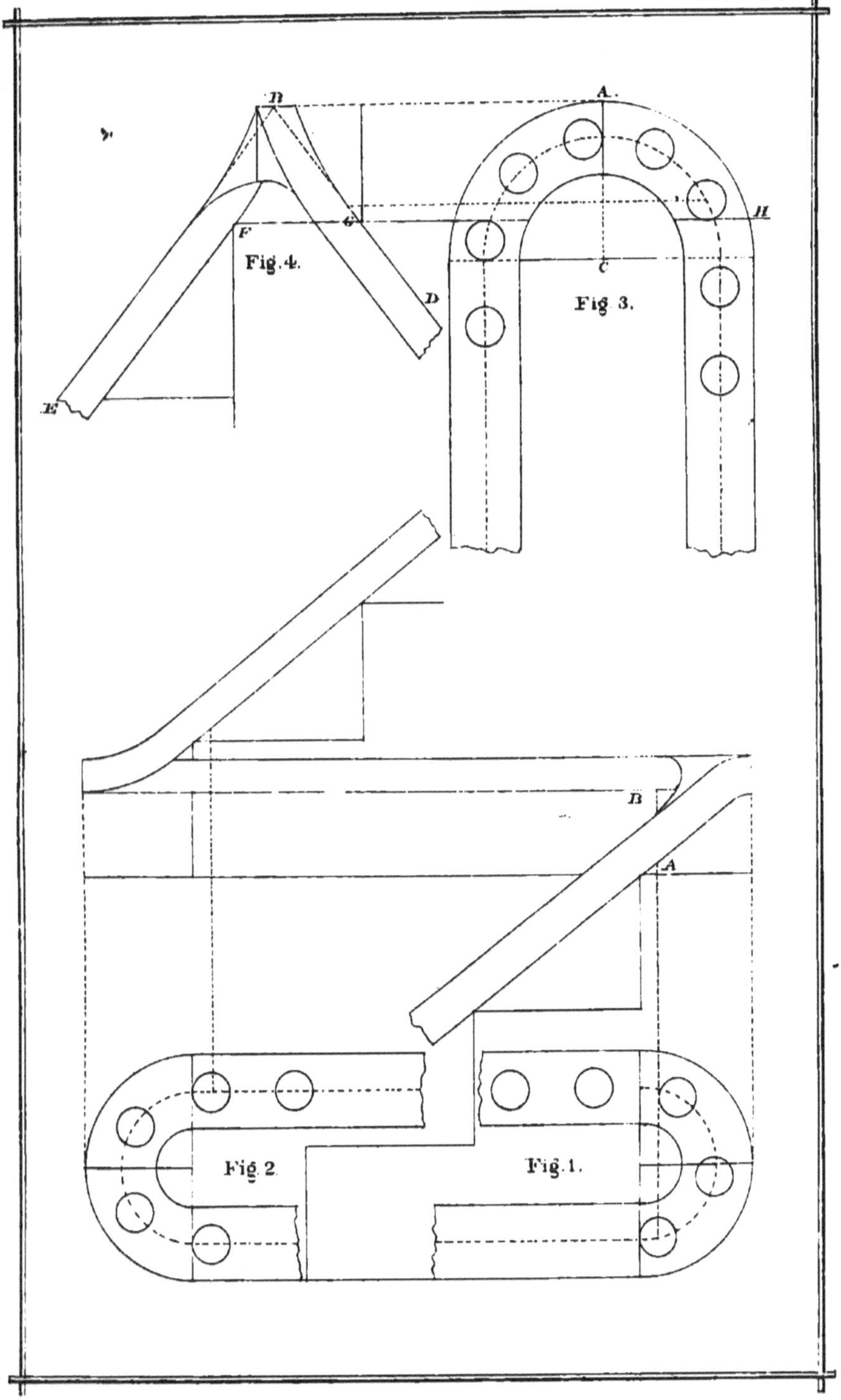

Plate 22.

Fig. 4.

Fig. 3.

Fig. 2.

Fig. 1.

## ADHESION OF GLUE.

Mr. Bevan glued together by the ends two cylinders of dry ash-wood, one-fifth of an inch diameter and about eight inches long; after they had been glued together 24 hours, they required a force of 1260 pounds to separate them; and as the area of the circular ends of the cylinders were 1.76 inches, it follows that the force of 715 pounds would be required to separate one square inch.

It is right to observe, that the glue used in this experiment was newly made, and the season very dry. For in some former experiments on this substance, made in the winter season, and upon some glue which had frequently made, with occasional additions of glue and water, he obtained a result of 350 to 560 pounds to the square inch.

The present experiment, however, was conducted upon a larger scale, and with greater care in the direction of the resultant force, so that it might be, as near as practicable, in a line passing at right angles through the centres of the surfaces in contact. The pressure was applied gradually, and was sustained two or three minutes before it separated.

Upon examining the separated surfaces, the glue appeared to be very thin, and did not entirely cover the wood, so that the actual adhesion of glue must be something greater than 715 pounds to the square inch.

Mr. Bevan also tried the lateral cohesion of fir-wood, from a Scotch fir of his own planting, cut down in the autumn, sawn into boards, and, at the time of experiment, quite dry and seasoned. The force required to separate the wood was 562 pounds to to the square inch; consequently, if two pieces of this wood had been well glued together, the wood would have yielded in its substance before the glue.

For a subsequent experiment, made on solid glue, the cohesive force was found to be 4000 pounds per square inch; from which it may be inferred, that the application of this substance as a cement is susceptible of improvement.

# ORNAMENTAL WORK.

## PLATE 23.

Exhibits the method of constructing a Corinthian truss. A represents the eye of its volute at large, with the centres numbered on which the curves are described. B and C are Geometrical views showing the front and side elevation. A careful inspection of which will enable the workman to construct one of any size he may require.

Plate 23

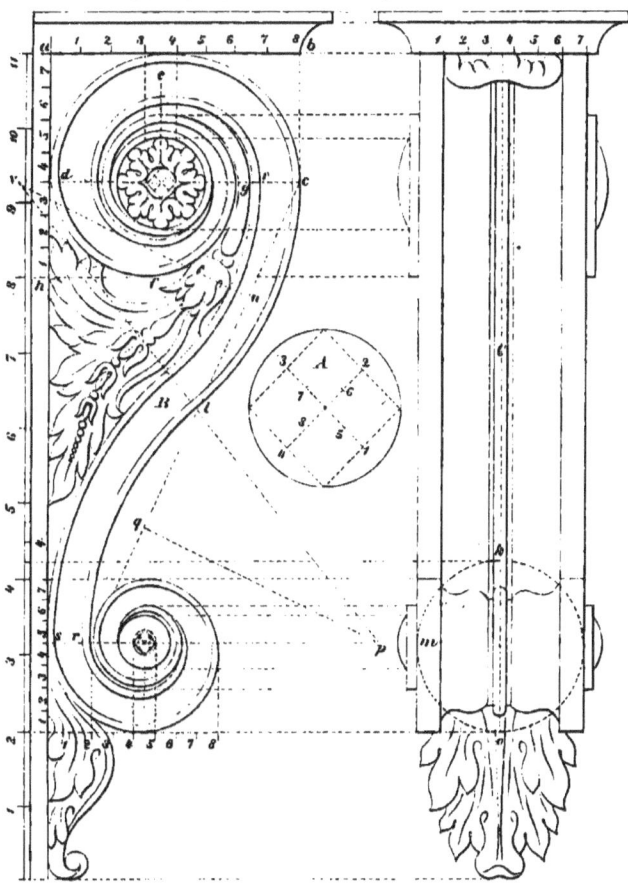

# A PRACTICAL AND MATHEMATICAL
# DEMONSTRATION

OF FINDING THE CIRCUMFERENCE AND SQUARING THE CIRCLE, WHEN THE DIAMETER IS GIVEN.

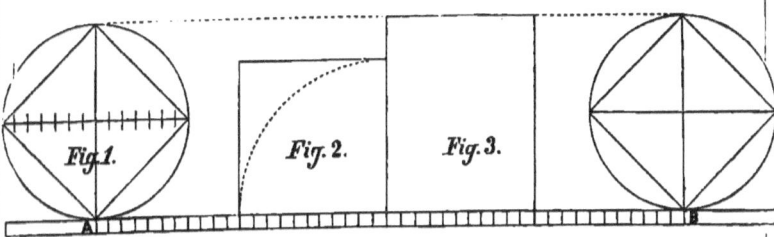

## RULES.

1. Eleven-fourteenth ($\frac{11}{14}$) of the diameter will give one-fourth ($\frac{1}{4}$) of the circumference.
2. One-fourth ($\frac{1}{4}$) of the circumference multiplied by the diameter will give the area of the circle.
3. Eleven-fourteenths ($\frac{11}{14}$) of the area of the circle will give the area of a square whose sides are equal to the circumference.
4. Seven-elevenths ($\frac{7}{11}$) of the area of the circle will give the area of an inscribed square.
5. One-quarter of the circumference multiplied by nine (9) will give the side of an inscribed square.
6. To find the diameter when the circumference is given, multiply by seven (7) and divide by twenty-two (22.)

To find the circumference and diameter when the area is given. Eleven-fourteenths ($\frac{11}{14}$) of the area gives the area of a square whose sides are equal to the circumference, the square root of which will give one-fourth of the circumference; to find the diameter, proceed as in rule 6.

The *Cut* represents a practical method of finding the circumference when the diameter is given:

Suppose Fig. 1 to be a wheel fourteen (14) feet or fourteen (14) inches in diameter, and A B the plane. Then with the point on the plane at A, roll the wheel over until the point at A strikes the plane

# 52 MATHEMATICAL DEMONSTRATION.

at B, which will be the circumference of the wheel. Then divide the distance on the plane between A and B into forty-four (44) parts, and fourteen (14) of those parts will be the exact diameter of the wheel, and eleven (11) of those parts will equal one-fourth ($\frac{1}{4}$) of the circumference, which is a practical demonstration and proves that eleven-fourteenths ($\frac{11}{14}$) of the diameter gives one-fourth ($\frac{1}{4}$) of the circumference.

A mathematical proof is that one-fourth ($\frac{1}{4}$) of the circumference multiplied by the diameter gives the area of the circle; seven elevenths ($\frac{7}{11}$) of the area of the circle will give the area of an inscribed square, as shown at Fig. 1; eleven-fourteenths ($\frac{11}{14}$) of the area of the circle gives the area of a square whose sides are equal to the circuference, as shown at Fig. 2.

And finally that a quadrialateral figure fourteen by eleven ($14 \times 11$) as shown in Fig. 3, is a square containing the same area as the circle; fourteen (14) being the diameter of the circle given and eleven (11) one-fourth of the circumference, which is squaring the circle, and its area.

These rules give the exact circumference of the circle in feet and inches where the diameters are 1, 2, 3, 4, etc. multiplied by 7, with as much certainty as you can find the root of a perfect number, and are original with me, but since their discovery I have learned that Archimedes, a celebrated Greek philosopher, discovered that eleven-fourteenths of the diameter gives one-fourth of the circumference, and had Archimedes given the practical and mathematical proofs of the fact which we claim to have done, they undoubtedly would have been adopted and in general use in all of our institutions of learning.

## Miscellaneous Rules.

The greatest force produced by the wind on a vertical wall, is equal to 40 lbs. to the square foot.

When a summer or beam has settled one fortieth of its length, it is liable to break.

Lathes for plastering will lay 48 feet to the bundle, equal to $5\frac{1}{3}$ square yards.

One barrel of lime to one cubic yard of sand, will plaster 17 square yards with two coats.

It requires 14 bricks to lay 1 foot in length and 1 foot in heighth of an 8 inch wall; 20 bricks for a 12 inch wall, and 27 bricks for a 16 inch wall.

An acre of ground is $208\frac{1}{2}$ feet square, and contains 43,560 square feet.

In water, sound passes 4,766 feet per second, in air, 1,146 feet per second.

A Winchester bushel is $18\frac{1}{2}$ inches in diameter, 8 inches deep, and contains $2150\frac{2}{5}$ cubic inches.

A box 16 x 16 inches square $8\frac{2}{5}$ inches deep will hold a bushel.

A box 12 x 12 inches square, $7\frac{1}{2}$ inches deep will hold half bushel.

A box 9 x 9 inches square, $6\frac{2}{5}$ inches deep will hold one peck.

A box 7 x 7 inches square $5\frac{1}{4}$ inches deep, will hold 4 qts. or half peck.

A pile of wood 8 feet long, and 4 feet high, contains 1 cord.

A cistern 5 feet diameter, and 6 feet deep, will hold 30 barrels, of 32 gallons each.

A cistern 6 feet diameter, and 6 feet deep, will hold 39 barrels.

A cistern 7 feet diameter, and 6 feet deep, will hold 54 barrels.

## MISCELLANEOUS RULES.

At the depth of 45 feet the temperature of the earth is uniform throughout the year.

Dimensions of drawings for patents in the United States, 8.5 × 12 inches.

The lap of slates varies from 2 to 4 inches; the standard is assumed to be 3 inches.

The pitch of a slate roof should not be less than 1 inch in height, to 4 inch in length.

According to the last census, there are 2,000 Architects, 350,000 Carpenters, 45,000 Cabinet makers, and 46,000 Carriage makers in the United States.

The strength of a horse is equivalent to that of 5 men, the daily allowance of water for a horse should be 4 gallons.

ELASTICTY AND STRENGTH.—The component parts of a rigid body adhere to each other with a force which is termed *Cohesion.*

Elasticty is the resistance which a body opposes to a change of form.

Strength is the resistance which a body opposes to a permanent separation of its parts.

A horse can draw upon a plank road three times the load that he can upon an ordinary broken stone or macadamized road.

### AMERICAN VALUATION OF FOREIGN MONEY.

A British pound sterling is increased from $4.84 to $4.86.65; the French, Swiss and Belgian francs from 18.06 to 19.03 with a similar increase on the Greek drachma and Spanish peseta. The Portuguese milreis will be decreased in valuation from $1.12 to $1.08.47.

# Terms Used in Carpentry.

ABUTMENT.—The junction or meeting of two pieces of timber, of which the fibres of the one extend perpendicular to the joint, and those of the other parallel to it.

ARRIS.—The line of concourse or meeting of two surfaces.

BACK OF A HAND-RAIL.—The upper side of it.

BACK OF A HIP.—The upper edge of a rafter, between the two sides of a hipped roof, formed to an angle, so as to range with the rafters on each side of it.

BACK-SHUTTERS OR BACK-FLAPS.—Additional breadths hinged to the front shutters for covering the aperture completely, when required to be shut.

BACK OF A WINDOW.—The board, or wainscoting between the sash-frame and the floor, uniting with the two elbows, and forming part of the finish of a room. When framed, it has commonly a single pannel, with mouldings on the framing, corresponding with the doors, shutters, &c., in the apartment in which it is fixed.

BASIL.—The sloping edge of a chisel, or of the iron of a plane.

BATTEN.—A scantling of stuff from two inches to seven inches in breadth, and from half an inch to one inch and a half in thickness.

BAULK.—A piece of fir or deal, from four to ten inches square, being the trunk of a tree of that species of wood, generally brought to a square, for the use of building.

BEAD.—A round moulding commonly made upon the edge of a piece of stuff. Of beads there are two kinds; one flush with the surface, called a *quirk-bead*, and the other raised, called a *cock-bead*.

BEAM.—A horizontal timber, used to resist a force or weight; as a *tie-beam*, where it acts as a string or chain, by its tension: as a *collar-beam*, where it acts by compression;

as a *bressummer*, where it resists a transverse insisting weight.

BEARER.—Any thing used by way of support to another.

BEARING.—The distance in which a beam or rafter is suspended in the clear: thus, if a piece of timber rests upon two opposite walls, the span of the void is called the *bearing*, and not the whole length of the timber.

BENCH.—A platform supported on four legs, and used for planing, upon etc.

BEVEL.—One side is said to be *bevelled* with respect to another, when the angle formed by these two sides is greater or less than a right angle.

BIRD'S MOUTH.—An interior angle, formed on the end of a piece of timber, so that it may rest firmly upon the exterior angle of another piece.

BLADE.—Any part of a tool that is broad and thin; as the blade of an axe, of an adze, of a chisel, &c.: but the blade of a saw is generally called the plate.

BLOCKINGS.—Small pieces of wood, fitted in, or glued, or fixed, to the interior angle of two boards or other pieces, in order to give strength to the joint.

BOARD.—A substance of wood contained between two parallel planes: as when the baulk is divided into several pieces by the pit-saw, the pieces are called *boards*. The section of boards is sometimes, however, of a triangular, or rather trapezoidal form; that is, with one edge very thin; these are called *feather-edge boards*.

BOND-TIMBERS.—Horizontal pieces, built in stone or brick walls, for strengthening them, and securing the battening, lath, and plaster, etc.

BOTTOM RAIL.—The lowest rail of a door.

BOXINGS OF A WINDOW.—The two cases, one on each side of a window, into which the shutters are folded.

BRACE.—A piece of slanting timber, used in truss-partitions, or in framed roofs, in order to form a triangle, and thereby rendering the frame immovable; when a brace is used by way of support to a rafter, it is called a *strut*. Braces, in partitions and spanroofs, are always, or should be, disposed in pairs, and placed in opposite directions.

BRACE AND BITS.—The same as *stock and bits*, as explained hereafter.

BRAD.—A small nail, having no head except on one edge. The intention is to drive it within the surface of the wood, by means of a hammer and punch, and to fill the cavity flush to the surface with putty.

BREAKING DOWN, in sawing, is dividing the baulk into boards or planks; but, if planks are sawed longitudinally, through their thickness, the saw-way is called a *ripping-cut* and the former a *breaking-cut*.

To BREAK-IN.—To cut or break a hole in brick-work, with the ripping-chisel, for inserting timber, etc.

BREAKING JOINT.—Is the joint formed by the meeting of several heading joints in one continued line, which is sometimes the case in folded doors.

BRESSUMMER OR BREASTSUMMER.—A beam supporting a superincumbent part of an exterior wall, and running longitudinally below that part.—SEE SUMMER.

BRIDGED GUTTERS.—Gutters made with boards, supported below with bearers, and covered over with lead.

BRIDGING-FLOORS.—Floors in which *bridging joists* are used.

BRIDGING JOISTS.—The smallest beams in naked flooring, for supporting the boarding for walking upon.

BUTTING-JOINT.—The junction formed by the surfaces of two pieces of wood, of which one surface is perpendicular to the fibres, and the other in their direction, or making with them an oblique angle.

CHAMBER.—The convexity of a beam upon the upper edge, in order to prevent its becoming straight or concave by its own weight, or by the burden it may have to sustain, in course of time.

CHAMBER-BEAMS.—Those beams used in the flats of truncated roofs, and raised in the middle with an obtuse angle, for discharging the rain-water towards both sides of the roof.

CANTALIVERS.—Horizontal rows of timber, projecting at right angles from the naked part of a wall, for sustaining the eaves or other mouldings. Sometimes they are planed on the horizontal and verticle sides, and sometimes the carpentry is rough and cased with joinery.

CARRIAGE OF A STAIR.—The timber-work which supports the steps.

CARCASE OF A BUILDING.—The naked walls, and the rough timber-work of the flooring and quarter partitions, before the building is plastered or the floors laid.

CARRY-UP.—A term used among builders or workmen, denoting that the walls, or other parts, are intended to be built to a certain given height; thus, the carpenter will say to the bricklayer, *Carry-up that wall ; carry-up that stack of chimneys*; which means, build up that wall or stack of chimneys.

CASTING OR WARPING.—The bending of the surfaces of a piece of wood from their original position, either by the weight of the wood, or by an unequal exposure to the weather or by unequal texture of the wood.

CHAMFERING.—Cutting the edge of any thing, originally right-angled, aslope or bevel.

CLAMP.—A piece of wood fixed to the end of a thin board, by mortise and tenon, or by groove and tongue; so that the fibres of the one piece, thus fixed, traverse those of the board, and by this mean prevent it from casting: the piece at the end is called a *clamp* and the board is said to be *clamped*.

CLEAR STORY WINDOWS, are those that have no transom.

CROSS-GRAINED STUFF, is that which has its fibres running in contrary positions to the surfaces ; and consequently, cannot be made perfectly smooth, when planed in one direction, without turning it, or turning the plane.

CROWN-POST.—The middle post of a trussed roof.—SEE KING-POST.

CURLING STUFF.—That which is occasioned by the winding or coiling of the fibres round the boughs of the tree, when they begin to shoot from the trunk.

DEAL TIMBER.—The timber of the fir-tree, as cut into boards, planks, etc., for the use of building.

DISCHARGE.—A post trimmed up under a beam, or part of a building which is weak or overcharged by weight.

DOOR-FRAME.—The surrounding case of a door, into which, and out of which, the door shuts and opens.

DORMER, OR DORMER WINDOW.—A projecting window, in the roof of a house; the glass-frame, or casements, being set vertically, and not in the inclined sides of the roofs: thus *dormers* are distinguished from *skylights*, which have their sides inclined to the horizon.

DRAG.—A door is said to *drag* when it rubs on the floor. This arises from the loosening of the hinges, or the settling of the building.

DRAGON-BEAM.—The piece of timber which supports the hip-rafter, and bisects the angle formed by the wall-plates.

DRAGON-PIECE.—A beam besecting the wall-plate, for receiving the heel or foot of the hip-rafters.

EDGING.—Reducing the edges of ribs or rafters, externally, or internally so as to range in a plane, or in any curved surface required.

ENTER.—When the end of a tenon is put into a mortise, it is said to *enter* the mortise.

FACE-MOULD.—A mould for drawing the proper figure of a hand-rail on both sides of the plank; so that, when cut by a saw, held at a required inclination, the two surfaces of the rail-piece, when laid in the right position, will be every where perpendicular to the plan.

FANG.—The narrow part of the iron of any instrument which passes into the stock.

FEATHER-EDGED BOARDS.—Boards, thicker at one edge than

the other, and commonly used in the facing of wooden walls, and for the covering of inclined roofs, etc.

FENCE OF A PLANE.—A guard which obliges it to work to a certain horizontal breadth from the arris.

FILLING-IN PIECES.—Short timbers less than the full length, as the jack-rafters of a roof, the puncheons or short quarters, in partitions, between braces and sills, or headpieces.

FINE-SET.—A plane is said to be fine-set, when the sole of the plane so projects as to take a very thin broad shaving.

FIR POLES.—Small trunks of fir trees, from ten to sixteen feet in length, used in rustic buildings and out-houses.

FREE STUFF.—That timber or stuff which is quite clean, or without knots, and works easily, without tearing.

FROWY STUFF.—The same as free stuff.

FURRINGS.—Slips of timber nailed to joists or rafters, in order to bring them to a level, and to range them into a straight surface, when the timbers are sagged, either by casting, or by a set which they have obtained by their weight, in length of time.

GIRDER.—The principal beam in a floor for supporting the binding-joists.

GLUE.—A tenacious viscid matter, which is used as a cement, by carpenters, joiners, etc.

Glues are found to differ very much from each other, in their consistence, color, taste, smell, and solubility. Some will dissolve in cold water, by agitation; while others are soluble only at the point of ebullition. The best glue is generally admitted to be transparent, and of a brown yellow color, without either taste or smell. It is perfectly soluble in water, forming a viscous fluid, which, when dry, preserves its tenacity and transparency in every part; and has solidity, color, and viscidity, in proportion to the age and strength of the animal from which it is produced. To distinguish good glue from bad, it is necessary to hold it between the eye and light; and if it appears of a strong dark brown color, and free from cloudy or black spots, it may be pronounced to be good. The best glue may likewise be known by immersing it in cold water for three or four days, and if it swells considerably without melting, and afterwards regains its former dimensions and properties by being dried, the article is of the best quality.

In preparing glue for use, it should be softened and swelled by steeping it in cold water for a number of hours. It should then be dissolved, by gently boiling it till it is of a proper consistence to be easily brushed over any surface. A portion of water is added to glue, to make it of a proper consistency, which portion may be taken at about a quart of water to half a pound of glue. In order to hinder the glue from being burned, during the process of boiling, the vessel containing the glue is generally suspended in another vessel, which is made of copper, and resembles in form a tea-kettle without a spout. This latter vessel contains only water, and alone receives the direct influence of the fire.

A little attention to the following circumstances will tend, in no small degree, to give glue its full effect in uniting perfectly two pieces of wood : first, that the glue be thoroughly melted, and used while boiling hot; secondly, that the wood be perfectly dry and warm ; and, lastly, that the surfaces to be united should be covered only with a thin coat of glue, and after having been strongly pressed together, left in a moderately warm situation, till the glue is completely dry. When it so happens that the face of surfaces to be glued cannot be conveniently compressed together in any great degree, they should, as soon as besmeared with the glue, be rubbed lengthwise, one on the other, several times, in order thereby to settle them close. When all the above circumstances cannot be combined in the same operation, the hotness of the glue and the dryness of the wood should at all events, be attended to.

The qualities of glue are often impaired by frequent meltings. This may be known to be the case when it becomes of a dark and almost black color ; its proper color being a light ruddy brown: yet, even then, it may be restored, by boiling it over again, refining it, and adding a sufficient quantity of fresh; but the fresh is seldom put into the kettle till what is in it has been purged by a second boiling.

If common glue be melted with the smallest possible quantity of water, and well mixed by degrees with linseed oil, rendered dry by boiling it with litharge, a glue may be obtained that will not dissolve in water. By boiling common glue in skimmed milk the same effect may be produced.

A small portion of finely levigated chalk is sometimes added to the common solution of glue in water, to strengthen it and fit it for standing the weather.

A glue that will resist both fire and water may be prepared by mixing a handful of quick lime with four ounces of linseed oil, thoroughly levigated, and then boiled to a good thickness, and kept in the shade, on tin-plates, to dry. It may be rendered fit for use by boiling it over a fire like common glue.

GRIND STONE.—A cylindrical stone, by which, on its being turned round its axis, edgetools are sharpened, by applying the basil to the convex surface.

GROUND-PLATE OR SILL.—The lowest plate of a wooden building for supporting the principal and other posts.

GROUNDS.—Pieces of wood concealed in a wall, to which the facings or finishings are attached, and having their surfaces flush with the plaster.

HANDSPIKE.—A lever for carrying a beam, or other body, the weights being placed in the middle, and supported at each end by a man.

HANGING STILE.—The stile of a door or shutter to which the hinge is fastened: also, a narrow stile fixed to the jamb on which a door or shutter is frequently hung.

HIP-ROOF.—A roof the ends of which rise immediately from the wall-plate, with the same inclination to the horizon, and its other two sides. The *Backing of a Hip* is the angle made on its upper edge to the range with the two sides or planes of the roof between which it is placed.

HOARDING.—An enclosure of wood about a building, while erecting or repairing.

JACK RAFTERS.—All those short rafters which meet the hips.

JACK RIBS.—Those short ribs which meet the angle ribs, as in groins, domes, etc.

JACK TIMBER.—A timber shorter than the whole length of other pieces in the same range.

INTER-TIE OR ENTER-TIE.—A horizontal piece of timber, framed between two posts, in order to tie them together.

JOGGLE-PIECE—A truss post, with shoulders and sockets for abutting and fixing the lower ends of the struts.

JOISTS.—Those beams in a floor which support, or are necessary in the supporting, of the boarding or ceiling; as the *binding, bridging* and *ceiling joists;* girders are, however, to be excepted, as not being joists.

JUFFERS.—Stuff of about four or five inches square, and of several lengths. This term is out of use, though frequently found in old books.

KERF.—The way which a saw makes in dividing a piece of wood into two parts.

KING-POST.—The middle post of a trussed roof, for supporting the tie-beam at the middle and the lower ends of the struts.

KNEE.—A piece of timber cut at an angle, or having grooves to an angle. In handrailing a *knee* is part of the back, with a convex curvature, and therefore the reverse of a *ramp*, which is hollow on the back, now called over or under easing.

KNOT.—That part of a piece of timber where a branch had issued out of the trunk.

LINING OF A WALL.—A timber, boarding, of which the edges are either rebated or grooved and tongued.

LINTELS.—Short beams over the heads of doors and windows, for supporting the inside of an exterior wall; and the super-incumbent part over doors, in brick or stone partitions.

LOWER RAIL.—The rail at the foot of a door next to the floor.

LYING PANEL.—A panel with the fibres of the wood disposed horizontally.

MARGINS OR MARGENTS.—The flat part of the stiles and rails of framed work.

MIDDLE RAIL.—The rail of a door which is upon a level with the hand when hanging freely and bending the joint of the wrist. The lock of the door is generally fixed in this rail.

MITRE.—If two pieces of wood be formed to equal angles, or if the two sides of each piece form an equal inclination, and two sides, one of each piece, be joined together at their common vertex, so as to make an angle, or an inclination, double to that of either piece, they are said to be *mitred* together, and the joint is called the *mitre*.

MORTISE AND TENON.—The tenon, in general, may be taken at about one-third of the thickness of the stuff.

When the mortise and tenon are to lie horizontally, as the juncture will thus be unsupported, the tenon should not be more than one-fifth of the thickness of the stuff; in order that the strain on the upper surface of the tenoned piece may not split off the under cheek of the mortise.

When the piece that is tenoned is not to pass the end of the mortised piece, the tenon should be reduced one-third or one-fourth of its breadth, to prevent the necessity of opening one side of the tenon. As there is always some danger of splitting the end of the piece in which the mortise is made, the end beyond the mortise should, as often as possible, be made considerably longer than it is intended to remain; so that the tenon may be driven tightly in, and the superfluous wood cut off afterwards.

But the above regulations may be varied, according as the tenoned or mortised piece is weaker or stronger.

The labor of making deep mortises, in hard wood, may be lessened, by first boring a number of holes with the auger, in the part to be mortised, as the compartments between may then more easily be cut away by the chisel.

Before employing the saw to cut the shoulder of a tenon, in neat work, if the line of its entrance be correctly determined by nicking the place with a paring chisel, there will be no danger of the wood being torn at the edges by the saw.

As the neatness and durability of a juncture depend entirely on the sides of the mortise coming exactly in contact with the sides of the tenon; and, as this is not easily performed when a mortise is to pass entirely through a piece of stuff, the space allotted for it should be first of all correctly gauged on both sides. One-half is then to be cut from one side, and the other half from the opposite side; and as any irregularities which may arise from an error in the direction of the chisel, will thus be confined to the middle of the mortise, they will be of very little hindrance to the exact fitting of the sides of the mortise and tenon. Moreover as the tenon is expanded by wedges after it is driven in, the sides of the mortise may, in a small degree, be inclined towards each other, near the shoulders of the tenon.

MULLION OR MUNNION.—A large vertical bar of a window-frame, separating two casements, or glass-frames, from each other.

Verticle *mullions* are called *munnions*; and those which extend horizontally are *transoms*.

MUNTINS OR MONTANTS.—The verticle pieces of the frame of a door between the stiles.

NAKED FLOORING.—The timber-work of a floor for supporting the boarding, or ceiling, or both.

NEWEL.—The post, in dog-legged stairs, where the winders terminate, and to which the adjacent string-boards are fixed.

9

OGEE.—A moulding, the transverse section of which consists of two curves of contrary flexure.

PANEL.—A thin board, having all its edges inserted in the groove of a surrounding frame.

PITCH OF A ROOF.—The inclination which the sloping sides make with the plane, or level of the wall-plate; or it is the proportion which arises by dividing the span by the height. Thus, if it be asked, What is the pitch of such a roof? the answer is, one-quarter, one-third, or half. When the pitch is half, the roof is a square, which is the highest that is now in use, or that is necessary in practice.

PLANK.—All boards above one inch thick are called *planks*.

PLATE.—A horizontal piece of timber in a wall, generally flush with the inside, for resting the ends of beams, joists or rafters, upon; and, therefore, denominated floor or roof plates.

POSTS.—All upright or vertical pieces of timber whatever; as *truss-posts*, *door-posts*, *quarters* in partitions, etc.

BRICK POSTS.—Intermediate posts in a wooden building, framed between principal posts.

PRINCIPAL POSTS.—The corner posts of a wooden building.

PUDLAIES.—Pieces of timber to serve the purpose of handspikes.

PUNCHIONS.—Any short post of timber. The small quarterings in a stud partition above the head of a door, are also called *Punchions*.

PURLINS.—The horizontal timbers in the sides of a roof, for supporting the spars or small rafters.

QUARTERING.—The stud work of a partition.

QUARTERS.—The timbers to be used in stud partitions, bond in walls, etc.

RAFTERS.—All the inclined timbers in the sides of a roof; as *principal rafters*, *hip rafters*, *and common rafters*; the latter are called in most countries, *spars*.

RAILS.—The horizontal pieces which contain the tenons in

a piece of framing, in which the upper and lower edges of the panels are inserted.

RAISING PLATES OR TOP PLATES.—The plates on which the roof is raised.

RANK-SET.—The edge of the iron of a plane is said to be *rank-set* when it projects considerably below the sole.

RETURN.—In any body with two surfaces, joining each other at an angle, one of the surfaces is said to *return* in respect of the other; or, if standing before one surface, so that the eye may be in a straight line with the other, or nearly so; this last is said to *return*.

RIDGE.—The meeting of the rafters on the vertical angle, or highest part of a roof.

RISERS.—The verticle sides of the steps of stairs.

ROOF.—The covering of a house; but the word is used in carpentry for the wood-work which supports the slating or other covering.

SCANTLING.—The transverse dimensions of a piece of timber; sometimes, also the small timbers in roofing and flooring are called *scantlings*.

SCARFING.—A mode of joining two pieces of timber, by bolting or nailing them transversely together, so that the two appear but as one. The joint is called a *scarf*, and timbers are said to be *scarfed*.

SHAKEN STUFF.—Such timber as is rent or split by the heat of the sun, or by the fall of the tree, is said to be *shaken*.

SHINGLES.—Thin pieces of wood used for covering, instead of tiles, etc.

SHREADINGS.—A term not much used at present.

SKIRTINGS OR SKIRTING BOARDS.—The narrow boards around the margin of a floor, forming a plinth for the base of the *dado*, or simply a plinth for the room itself, when there is no dado.

SKIRTS OF A ROOF.—The projecture of the eaves.

SLEEPERS.—Pieces of timber for resting the ground-joists

of a floor upon, or for fixing the planking to, in a bad foundation. The term formerly applied to the *valley rafters* of a roof.

SPARS.—A term by which the common rafters of a roof are best known in almost every provincial town in Great Britain; though, generally, called in London *common rafters*, in order to distinguish them from the principal rafters.

STAFF.—A piece of wood fixed to the external angle of the two upright sides of a wall, for floating the plaster to, and for defending the angle against accidents.

STILES OF DOOR, are the verticled arts of the framing at the edges of the door.

STRUTS.—Pieces of timber which support the rafters, and which are supported by the truss-posts.

SUMMER.—A large beam in a building, either disposed in an outside wall, or in the middle of an apartment, parallel to such wall. When a *summer* is placed under a superincumbent part of an outside wall, it is called a *bressummer*, as it comes in abrest with the front of the building.

SURBASE.—The upper base of a room, or rather the cornice of the pedestal of the room, which serves to finish the dado, and to secure the plaster against accidents from the back of chairs and other furniture on the same level.

TAPER.—The form of a piece of wood which arises from one end of a piece being narrower than the other.

TENON.—SEE MORTISE.

TIE.—A piece of timber, placed in any position, and acting as a string or tie, to keep two things together which have a tendency to a more remote distance form each other.

TRANSOM WINDOWS.—Those windows which have horizontal mullions.

TRIMMERS.—Joists into which other joists are framed.

TRIMMING JOISTS.—The two joists into which a trimmer is framed.

TRUNCATED ROOF.—A roof with a flat on the top.

TRUSS.—A frame constructed of several pieces of timber,

and divided into two or more triangles by oblique pieces, in order to prevent the possibility of its revolving round any of the angles of the frame.

TRUSSED ROOF.—A roof so constructed within the exterior triangular frame, as to support the principal rafters and the tie-beam at certain given points.

TRUSS-POST.—Any of the posts of a trussed roof, as a *king-post*, *queen-post*, or *side-post*, or posts into which the braces are formed in a trussed partition.

TRUSSELLS.—Four-legged stools for ripping and cross-cutting timber upon.

TUSK.—The bevelled upper shoulder of a tenon, made in order to give strength to the tenon.

UPHERS.—Fir-poles, from twenty to forty feet long, and from four to seven inches in diameter, commonly hewn on the sides, so as not to reduce the wane entirely. When slit they are frequently employed in slight roofs: but mostly used whole for scaffolding and ladders.

VALLEY RAFTER.—That rafter which is disposed in the internal angle of a roof.

WALL PLATES.—The joint-plates and raising plates.

WEB OF AN IRON.—The board part of it which comes to the sole of the plane.

## PLASTERER'S WORK.

The *measuring* and *valuation* of plasterer's work is conducted by surveyors. All common plastering is measured by the yard square, of nine feet; this includes the partitions and ceilings of rooms, stuccoing, internally and externally, etc., etc. Cornices are measured by the foot superficial, girting their members to ascertain their widths, which multiplied by their lengths, will produce the superficial contents. Running measures consist of beads, quirks, arrises, and small mouldings. Ornamental cornices are frequently valued in this way; that is, by the running foot.

The labor in plasterer's work is frequently of more consideration than the materials; hence it becomes requisite to note down the exact time which is consumed in effecting particular portions, so that an adequate and proper value may be put upon the work.

# "Achenor"--Its Meaning.

Of old, the wise man said: "There is nothing new under the sun." Each succeeding age has echoed it—even this nineteenth century, perforce, joining the strain.

Do we chant our triumph in art, in science; do we exult in the advance in the science of government—hailing the "rings" that govern us, and plunder us, as the very last and greatest achievement in human progress; turn back the pages of history and we find a record which compels us to say, "The thing that is, it is that that has been."

What wonder, then, if even this boast of our age, the self-feeding principle as applied to Furnaces, &c., should have been known and used by them of old!

And we so read of a "Furnace, 1800 years ago, having a tower or magazine suspended over the fire-chamber, for the purpose of furnishing a constant supply of fuel, thus obtaining a perpetual fire."

Hence it was called, in the Greek, "Athanor," "Acanor," or "Achenor," signifying "deathless," "undying."

But herein is a difference between us and those of the bygone days, and one which well illustrates the difference in our civilization.

The old Achenor Furnaces were used by the alchemists, in their vain efforts to transmute the baser metals into gold—in their fruitless search after the "philosopher's stone."

The new Achenor Furnaces seek the promotion of health of mind, and well-being of body, a treasure richer far than the "Midas" power sought of old.

It is, then, an "old friend with a new face" we present in

and we are confident that they will inherit the name, because

1. An undying fire can be kept;
2. They are entirely free from deadly gases;
3. Their career, we believe, will be undying.

---

This matter of heating our homes is of such vital importance that we feel warranted in presenting in detail the more important features of the Achenor Furnaces, premising that they are not an untested experiment, but a tried and successful fact.

FOR SALE BY

## W. H. DRUMMOND & CO.,

85 and 87 MARKET ST., NEWARK, N. J.

# Gould's Patent Fire-Proof Hot Air Flues,

## FOR BUILDINGS, &c., &c.

## NO IRON LATHES NOR COMPLICATED CONTRIVANCES REQUIRED.

### Absolutely Fire-Proof---No Loss of Heat.

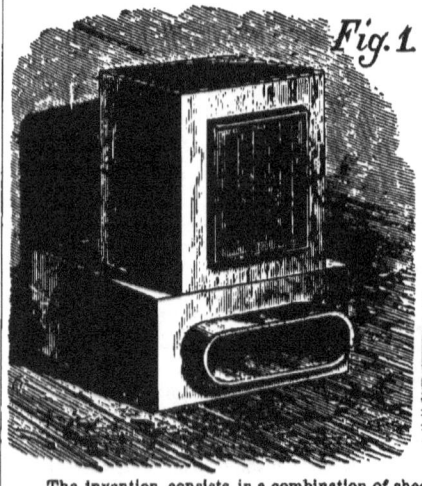
Fig. 1.

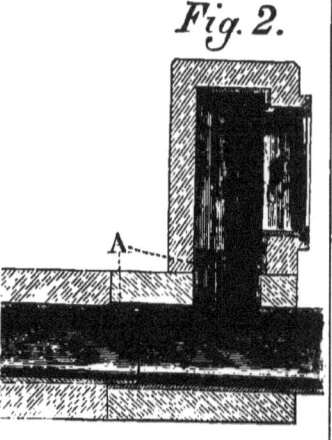
Fig. 2.

The invention consists in a combination of sheet tin tubes with Plaster of Paris, the tubes forming the lining of the manufactured article when completed. It will be seen that the combination of the plate-tin and Plaster of Paris is based upon sound scientific principles, when it is understood that the object of the invention is to prevent escape of the heat through the walls of the flues during the passage of the heated air from the furnace to the delivery register. Bright plate-tin, though a good reflector, is a very poor radiator of heat while Plaster of Paris is one of the best non-conductors.

The engravings will almost explain themselves. They represent one of the forms in which the flues may be made, these forms being practically unlimited, and capable of adaption to any of the requirements of such flues. Fig. 1 is a perspective view of a composite register box, and Fig. 2 is a geometrical section of the same, in which the shape of the tin lining in transverse section is that of a flattened cylinder. The sections of tin are much larger at one end than at the other; they can, therefore, be joined without cracking the plaster which is upon the outside. These tubes can be made so cheaply, and they are evidently such perfect security against fire originating in flues, that they ought to attract the attention of builders at once. It is also in harmony with the Building Laws of the State New York, as will be seen by the following extract :

*Extract from Laws of the State of New York, in relation to Building.*

HOT-AIR PIPES—No tin or other metal pipes or flues of metal, to convey heated air, shall be allowed, unless the same shall have a thickness of not less than one inch of Plaster of Paris between the said metal pipes or flues, and any of the timber of wood-work adjoining the same If the Plaster of Paris is not put on as above set forth, the pipes in all cases, must be doubled, that is to pipes, one inside the other, at least one inch apart and filled with Plaster of Paris.

### REFERENCES:

R. P. VAN RIPER, Montclair,
J. R. THOMPSON, Office Warren st.,
    Jersey City, Residence, Montclair,
JEROME SIGLER, Montclair,
A. A. SIGLER, Montclair,
FRED. BRAUTIGAN, Montclair,

H. HUDSON HOLLY, Architect, Trinity
    Buildings, N. Y.
JOSEPH DODD, Architect, Orange,
THOMAS STENT, Architect, Newark.
C. GRAHAM, Architect, Elizabeth.
BRIGGS & COLMAN, Architects, Newark.
HUGH LAMB, Architect, Newark.

### PRICES.

3x8 Inches, per Foot 80 Cts.    3x10 Inches, per Foot    90
3x9   "   "   "   85  "    3x12  "   "   "   $1.00

Register Boxes ready to receive Register according to size, either for Side Wall or Floor. No Soapstone Border required when these boxes are used. Address all orders to

## E. T. GOULD, Montclair, N. J.

# Bailey, Crane & Webster,

**WHOLESALE AND RETAIL DEALERS IN**

## Pine, Ash, Walnut and White Wood

# Lumber,

Yards, { Foot of Bridge St., Newark,
Passaic Ave., East Newark, N. J.

WM. F. BAILEY,  C. G. CRANE,  WM. H. WEBSTER.

ORNAMENTAL NEWEL POSTS AND BALUSTERS MADE TO ORDER.

## JOHN MIDDLETON,
# STAIR BUILDER,
### NO. 120 BERGEN ST., NEWARK, N. J.

Stairs and Rails Executed with Neatness and Dispatch.

ORDERS BY MAIL PROMPTLY ATTENDED TO.

---

### BRITTAIN'S
### COMBINED, ELECTRIC, BURGLAR AND FIRE
# ALARM,
#### IS SIMPLE, PERFECT AND GUARANTEED,
### MUST BE SEEN TO BE APPRECIATED.

No charge made until after a trial. Is put in quickly, no carpets taken up. It costs less than any other Alarm in the market—Is very popular.

*Call and see it, or address for particulars,*

### R. J. BRITTAIN,
#### No. 120 Bergen St., Newark, N. J.

Our Batteries are not offensive, and last one year without attention.
COST 30 CTS. PER ANNUM.

---

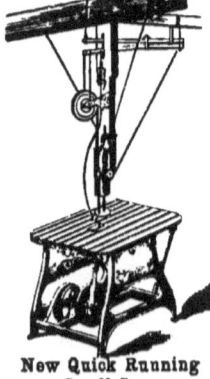

New Quick Running Scroll Saw.

### SMITH'S
# Wood Working Machinery

For Planing, Sash, and Moulding Mills,

### LOW PRICES,
### SUPERIOR QUALITY,
### EASY TERMS.

—ALSO—

### MACHINISTS' TOOLS.
### STEAM ENGINES, BOILERS, SHAFTING,

AND COMPLETE OUTFITS FOR FACTORIES.

## WRIGHT & SMITH,
#### Warerooms, 119 Liberty Street, New York.

FACTORY, NEWARK, N. J.    SEND FOR CIRCULARS.

## MEEKER & HEDDEN,
### BUILDERS,
### SASH, BLIND AND DOOR MANUFACTURERS,

Hardwood Doors, Mantels, Church, Bank and Office Furniture,

### WOOD MOULDINGS,

Scroll and Circular Sawing, Wood Turning, &c., &c.,

### OGDEN STREET, FOOT OF ORANGE,

J. J. MEEKER,
V. J. HEDDEN. }  **NEWARK, N. J.**

---

## ROMER & CO.,
### MANUFACTURERS OF
### BRASS PAD LOCKS,
### Builders and Bronze Hardware,
OF EVERY DESCRIPTION. ALSO,

Piano, Melodeon and Sewing Machine Locks, Brass and Composition Castings Made to Order,

### 141 AND 145 RAILROAD AVENUE,

C. W. A. ROMER,
J. H. WILKINS. }  **NEWARK, N. J.**

---

## SCRIMSHAW PAVEMENT
### For Streets, Carriage Houses and Drives,
### STABLE FLOORS, SIDE AND GARDEN WALKS,

It is now admitted to be the best Pavement in use. See the Pavement in front of the Industrial Exhibition Buildings. Call for testimonials, and leave orders at the

### Office, 766 Broad Street, Newark, N. J.
### ALSO, BUELL'S IMPROVED ARTIFICIAL STONE.

A. P. CORY.

---

## E. B. HOTCHKISS,
### MANUFACTURER OF
## PAPER BOXES,
OF EVERY DESCRIPTION, ALSO DEALER IN

Paper, Fancy Boxes, Paste Boards, and Fancy Articles,

### 878 AND 880 BROAD STREET,
**NEWARK, N. J.**

## MINTON'S TILES,

PLAIN AND ENCAUSTIC,

**For Public Buildings & Dwellings,**

AS LAID BY US IN

THE CAPITOL AT WASHINGTON,

In numerous Churches, Banks, and Dwellings in every part of the country.

### Glazed and Enameled Tiles

For Mantels, Hearths, Wainscoting, &c. and for Exterior Decoration.

**GARNKIRK CHIMNEY TOPS,**

PLUMBERS' MATERIALS, &c.

### MILLER & COATES,

**279 Pearl Street,**

NEW YORK.

---

## A. S. CARLE,

**Wood Turning,**

And Scroll Sawing Mills,

**Cor. High St., and Seventh Avenue,**

NEWARK, N. J.

Circular Mouldings a Specialty, any size up to 12 feet.

**Stair and Stoop Balusters,**

Newels, Shelf Columns, Line and Hitching Posts, Constantly on Hand.

All kinds of Work done at Short Notice.

Orders may be left at Builders' Exchange, 847 Broad St.

---

### ESTABLISHED IN 1848.

## MACKNET, WILSON & CO.,

IMPORTERS AND DEALERS IN

**Hardware, Iron and Steel,**

**MACHINE BELTING, STEAM PACKING, &C.**

**Builders' Hardware a Specialty,**

*No. 796 Broad Street,*

NEWARK, N. J.

THEO. MACKNET,
THOS. B. SMITH,

ORSON WILSON,
ELIAS B. CRANE.

www.ingramcontent.com/pod-product-compliance
Lightning Source LLC
Chambersburg PA
CBHW020135170426
43199CB00010B/747